More than 100

Spells
in the
City

More than 100 Spells in the City

Witchcraft for the modern world

Tudorbeth

Tudorbeth © 2013

All rights reserved.
No parts of this publication may be reproduced, stored in a retrieval system, or transmitted in any form or by any means whatsoever without the prior permission of the publisher.

A record of this publication is available from the British Library.

ISBN 978-1-907203-70-1

Typesetting by Wordzworth Ltd
www.wordzworth.com

Cover design by Titanium Design Ltd
www.titaniumdesign.co.uk

Printed by Lightning Source UK
www.lightningsource.com

Cover images by Nigel Peace

Published by Local Legend
www.local-legend.co.uk

Dedicated to my Uncle Denis, who inspires me constantly with his respect and love to endure the prejudice that society sends our way with strength and a beautiful sense of humour.

Blessed Be to all those who follow our ways.

About this book

There are few subjects that have attracted, in equal measure, as much prejudice and misconception as witchcraft. It has endured fear, scorn and even, in recent years, glorification in novels and films.

Yet in truth the Craft is simple and, literally, down to earth. It has a reverence for nature and an enduring place in all our hearts and minds. Who has not lit a candle for a loved one, or offered up a devout wish for some important event? Who has not believed in some lucky charm or spoken an affirmation? We are all practitioners of the Craft!

So would you like to know how to do it properly, with real natural power and intent, and to get results?

In this ground-breaking book, Tudorbeth opens up the traditional secrets of spell-weaving, and adapts them for our busy modern lives with clarity and simplicity. The ancient knowledge is offered to us here as never seen before.

Tudorbeth is a hereditary practitioner of the Craft. The rules and gifts of herb lore, scrying, healing, tasseomancy, numerology and candle magic have been passed down to her through several Celtic and English generations. Born in Wiltshire, she has an Honours degree in Religious Studies and has lived and worked in California and Italy, before returning to live in north London.

Previous Publications

The Craft in the City (ISBN 978-1-907203-43-5)

The Witch in the City (ISBN 978-1-907203-63-3)

www.local-legend.co.uk

To come in this series

Magic in the City

Spirit in the City

Contents

Introduction	1
The Bare Necessities	5
Love	9
Money	35
Career	53
Family	69
Health	85
Black and White Magic	101
Spells for the Seasons of the Year	103
The Last Word	107
Publications in this Series	109

Introduction

Dear Reader,

In this book we look at the art of spell-weaving and spell casting. I will show you how to use correspondences and to create your own spells on the five central themes in a person's life: love, money, health, family and career. There are about twenty spells for each theme.

You will also learn one of the oldest spells in the world, the 'candle and needle' spell, which can be used for any purpose you wish.

I will describe spells for each festival of nature in the year. These festival days are very powerful for us and if we tap into their energy we can boost our spells' power. Always remember that spells will come to you at the right time. They are influenced by your feelings and needs, and by the desired outcomes. Therefore, with spell-weaving everything needs to be in its right place and at its right time.

Spells are like prayers, with the added kick of using nature to fuel them. Our good intentions are cast out of us onto the breath of the air and sent through the universe. They are always for good, for healing and for giving and receiving that which we desire without bending the will of another or of any living presence.

If you wish to 'hex', or want to bend someone's will to your own, then this is not the book for you! Hexing is not what witchcraft is about. We do not cast ill will onto anyone. All that we wish for will return to us three-fold! (Although, if you feel that someone has hexed you, I shall show you the ways to deal with this and achieve a favourable outcome.)

When casting a love spell, for example, it is not about making someone choose you instead of being with someone else. The only spell you could cast in this instance is a 'clarity of mind' spell, so that the someone may see their situation clearly; but if this spell proves that they do not choose you, then you must move on, wish them luck and let go. A clarity of mind spell is a helping, healing spell, not a 'You will come to me' spell! Please always remember our code:

> An' it harm none, do what ye will.

'None' means every living being - we do not harm anything. This cannot be stressed enough; it is our good intentions, right thought, right mind and right action that bring results. The issue of black and white magic will be discussed later in this book. There has been, and continues to be, a great debate concerning this.

Many of the spells written here ask for the help of a particular deity. However, if you do not adhere to any gods then it's not important, you may just omit the name of the deity and replace it with 'the universe'. After all, we are working for external help. All of the spells can be rewritten to suit your own individual needs and feelings. If you do so, then write your spells down in a journal or diary, creating your own 'recipe book' or Book of Shadows. It is the beginning of your life in magic and something that can be passed on to future generations.

In this book you will also find some spells that will draw on the magic of the elementals, the magical beings such as dragons and leprechauns. Leprechauns are the elementals of the earth and dragons, of course, are the elementals of fire.[1] Some may say that such beings do not exist. However, they also say that witches do not exist, but here we are, alive and well in the twenty-first century! Maybe we're not in the form that such people would imagine – we're actually quite normal – and the same is true of leprechauns and dragons. You will learn how to call upon their power in the 'Wealth' chapter, due to what they represent.

Finally, this book will describe some of the fundamental ways to make essential items for spell-weaving such as oils, essential oils and elixirs (explaining the differences between food oils and essential oils) and what they can be used for.

Just a word of warning regarding spell-weaving… Spells can sometimes take on a meaning of their own and they can play out in a day, a week, a month or even years. So always be careful what you cast for!

Blessed Be

---

[1] A fuller description of all the elementals can be found in *Spirit in the City*.

The Bare Necessities

Dear Reader,

We shall take this opportunity to describe some basic essentials before we begin delving into the Famous Five of love, money, health, family and career, and their corresponding spells and charms.

As I have written in *The Craft in the City* and *The Witch in the City*, the Craft is not meant to be difficult or costly. Do not make it any more complicated than it has to be, and that includes the resources that we may need at times. You do not need to go to great extremes to make something if you haven't got the time or the space for it. You do not have to pay large amounts of money for any articles or ingredients required for a spell. YOU yourself have all the power needed to achieve the outcome of your own spell. You can manifest all that you seek. I will merely show you one way, but the Craft may come to you in different ways. Always trust your own instincts and be your own guide.

As we are not bound by any doctrine, only personal responsibility, the Craft and witches can take on new forms and adapt to whatever diverse challenges the world sends our way. Three hundred years ago, we were not concerned with global warming or recycling our rubbish. Less than fifty years ago, homosexuality was illegal in the UK. Gradually, the world changes and as witches we change with it. So here, for example, you will find love spells for all kinds of couples; love never changes, although the correspondences for each spell need to reflect those who are weaving it.

Let us look at some of the bare necessities of spell-weaving.

Many spells call for us to anoint a candle, which means to rub some of the stated essential oil onto the candle, including its sides and base. You can buy essential oils in all different varieties and quantities on the Internet, and it's certainly easier to buy them that way than to make them yourself. However, if you would like to try making scented oils from flowers and herbs, here are two methods that have basically not changed from ancient times. One is the cold steeping method, the other is over a double boiler or a bowl in a saucepan of water (similar to the process of candle-making[2]).

The latter involves simmering 50g of dried herbs in half a litre of oil for four hours in the double boiler, then carefully straining the oil and allowing it to cool before bottling. If making an essential oil use almond, jojoba or rapeseed oil. (I will use almond or jojoba oil, depending on the gender it will be used for.) Always write the date on a name label for the bottle in case you forget when you made it, as all things eventually lose their vitality. However, this method is very time consuming and also very much drains our natural energy; in other words, it is not only using our own energies but also our gas and electricity.

Therefore I recommend another method, less expensive on natural resources. Take a glass bottle and half fill it with oil, then cram as much of the plant material you can into it (flowers or herbs, or for example lettuce if making lettuce oil). Then put the lid on the bottle and let it sit for twenty-four hours in a cool, dark place. After this, shake it thoroughly and leave it for another three days before straining and putting the liquid into a dark glass container with a lid and a name and date label as before. This oil will now last for about six months, for spell work or as massage oil.

---

[2] See *The Craft in the City* for instructions on this.

Do not go to great expense buying fancy glass bottles for your oils. Save your jam jars and coffee jars! Wash them out and leave them until completely dry. Use glass paint to colour them darkly, such as in navy blue or deep dark red. You could colour-code them: red for essential oils and blue for oils to be used in cooking. You could also use medicine bottles when they're empty, as many of them are a dark brown colour. But make sure they're thoroughly washed and cleaned - leave them overnight in a bowl of boiling water with sea salt and about five or six slices of lemon in it. Lemon is a natural cleanser and you can use it on almost anything; nature always gives us an answer, even for our own dirt!

A word of warning regarding making food oils: be sure that the herb or plant material you are working with is not toxic, and is safe to be used in food. If you are unsure, however, as previously mentioned you could always buy these oils from speciality or health food shops, or on the Internet.

Further, always check with a medical practitioner before using oils if you are pregnant, have epilepsy or an allergy. Never use them neat on your skin (for massage, always use about ten drops of the base oil specified in a spell), and do not take them internally unless stated. Also be careful with sunlight after using oils as some are photosensitive. The best advice is to trust your instincts and knowledge, and when in doubt do not do it - whatever it is!

You will probably adapt some of the spells in this book to your own circumstances and write them in your own words. For this, I think the mnemonic Be SMART is a good guide:

S = specific and simple
M = measurable and meaningful
A = attainable and action-focused
R = relevant and results-orientated
T = timely and 'trackable'

If you try to Be SMART when you are spell-weaving then you will not stray too far from the path. It is a guide that is easy to follow. Another mnemonic I like and use is KISS, for Keep It Simple, Stupid!

Blessed Be

Love

Dear Reader,

In this letter we are going to look at the nature of love and the corresponding elements and components that can be used to induce love.

The best-known goddess of love is of course Aphrodite, or Venus, though each culture has a god or goddess that pertains to love. So you may wish to research the gods and goddesses of love in your own tradition.

In the west the most famous figure of love is Cupid (or Eros). He adorns Valentine's Day cards, and with his bow and arrow strikes love in the hearts of those he aims at. Yet the story of Cupid is not without trials and tribulations, a wise and cautionary tale regarding love, perhaps. His mother Venus was jealous of the princess Psyche and ordered her son to strike her with one of his golden arrows so that she would fall in love with the most disgusting being in the world. Unfortunately Cupid accidently pricked himself with his own arrow while in Psyche's room as she slept and, on seeing her, Cupid fell deeply in love with her. So he visited Psyche every night while she slept and told her that she mustn't ever see him; however, bated by her sisters, she did look at him and became tortured by love for him.

An angry Cupid fled and Psyche sought him all over the world. Venus relented and told Psyche she would help her to locate Cupid - after she had completed several tasks that of course, these being gods, became more difficult each time. As the final task, Psyche was ordered to give Hades, the ruler of the Underworld, a box containing eternal sleep. But naturally, like Pandora, curiosity got the better of Psyche who just had to open it...

By now, Cupid was no longer angry with Psyche so he rescued her and brought her back from eternal sleep. Psyche was made immortal so that she could spend eternity with Cupid and together they had a daughter, Voluptas. This is a lovely story and it does have a happy ending... eventually!

The path of true love never runs smooth. There are many hidden meanings within this story and one of the most important for the experience of love relates to the names involved: the name Cupid means 'desire' and Psyche means 'the soul'. Thus the eternal soul and pure desire come together to create Voluptas, meaning 'pleasure'! The symbolism within the story of Cupid and Psyche epitomises what we experience in love; it challenges our spirit and can wound and inflame the heart. It is also a wonderful and empowering thing, not to be treated lightly or with false motives.

It is the one request that witches are always asked about. So let's look at some of the correspondences to be used primarily when working love magic.

What do you know already? The colours you would automatically associate with love are pink and red, the flowers are of course roses, the crystal is the rose quartz and the oils might be lavender or jasmine. Yet there is so much more to this kind of magic and we need to use all the appropriate correspondences in order to create the right vibrations for the desired effects and outcomes. There are different forms of love, too, so here you will find spells regarding men seeking women, women seeking men, men seeking men and women seeking women.

There are some correspondences for love that are generic while others are more specific. For example, red candles represent health, energy, strength, courage and sexual potency, while pink candles are for love, affection and romance. Moreover, some spells and charms are generic, which means they can be used for all those who are seeking love or wish to enhance the love they have. One delightful such charm is this:

The Charm of Love
2 cinnamon sticks
1 tsp anise oil
1 tsp honey
2 drops musk oil
Rose petals
A pinch of catnip

Mix the oils, honey and catnip together and then soak the cinnamon sticks in the mixture with the rose petals for a couple of hours before leaving them to dry. Tie the cinnamon sticks together with red ribbon and hang them up in a place where you desire love to be. You can tie rose petals in with the cinnamon sticks also if you wish.

If you count the number of ingredients used in this charm, it comes to six. Six is the number of love (and also of responsibility), whereas nine is the number of romance (and also of artistic genius). However, a lot of the spells I will describe here will feature six or use six quantities.

By the way, there are a number of spells that have catnip in them. It's not just for cats! Catnip is a cooling, sedative herb that can soothe the digestion and help bring down a fever. If you have a garden, I suggest growing it; it is an aromatic mint plant with white flowers, and perfect for use in spells and charms for happiness and love.

General food aphrodisiacs, accredited with the power of sexual excitement, are celery, asparagus and mushrooms, while ginger, garlic, peppers, vanilla, cloves, borage and rue are herbs and spices that can also be effective. In addition, lavender, oysters, chocolate and rosemary are basic aphrodisiac compounds.

But the key ingredient with any love spell or charm is always *desire*. Yes, we are back to Cupid again. Indeed, throughout this letter references will be made to 'the Cupids', the beings of love, the messengers responsible for bringing together people who have a chance of love. Please notice the words 'a chance of love'. There is no point casting a love spell if your heart is closed and you really do not want anyone. You have to make room for love and show the universe that you are open to love. We are not talking about carpeting the house in rose petals and painting every room pink! But introduce little touches signifying that love could dwell in this house - an ornament of a heart, or a heart-shaped box is sufficient. You could make room in the wardrobe or set aside a drawer for someone, and start living as if there were two people in the house. When you make a meal, make enough for two and freeze a portion if it's not used. It is all about changing your attitude and shifting your consciousness to the next level, thinking of being a couple.

A sweet that can be made when cooking for your intended is suggested here. It is a wonderfully versatile dish and quick to make, but as you make it remember to infuse it with the key ingredient - the desire of how you want the night or day to be.

Chocolate Avocado Mousse
1 avocado
1 hot chocolate mix
(or about 3 - 4 tablespoons of pure cocoa powder)

Peel and quarter a ripe avocado, removing the stone, and chop it up into cubes. Place the ingredients together in a blender or hand mixer and blend them until smooth and no dry cocoa powder remains. Then pour it into dishes and store them in the fridge. This can be made a day in advance but do not leave it for more than a day. There are many other ingredients you could add to it: chocolate chips, cinnamon, ginger, bananas, a teaspoon of instant coffee for a mocha taste, coconut, nuts, a tablespoon of lavender liquor - the possibilities are endless. You could melt a bar of chocolate and pour this over the dish for pure decadence. It all depends on your budget, taste and imagination.

I should say a few words concerning Valentine's Day. This occurs on the 14th of February, which just happens to be the Roman fertility festival of Lupercalia. This festival lasted from February 13th to 15th. It was a much respected festival as it partly honoured Lupa, the she-wolf who suckled Romulus and Remus, the founders of Rome. The Luperci, or brothers of the wolf, would strike young women with thongs cut from the skins of sacrificed animals in order to ensure fertility and ease childbirth. It's rather a far cry from the day we know that honours Valentine, a Roman saint who was martyred for performing secret Christian weddings for soldiers who were forbidden to marry. Yet there are actually many saints' days of love. The day of love was traditionally March 12th, Saint Gregory's day, while the actual saint of love is Saint Anthony, who interestingly is also the saint of lost things (including people!).

There are a number of magical things we can do on a special day to invoke love. The first is the creation of magic love salt. If a full moon happens to occur on February 14th, this is a very rare and auspicious occasion so we must use it.

Magic love salt
Fill a bowl with sea salt and place it in view of the full moon (it can be inside on a window ledge) on February the 14th. The full moon has to occur exactly on that date. As you do so, say these words:

> *Goddess Venus, hear my plea,*
> *Send your strength of love to me.*
> *Let love travel through moon's rays,*
> *Graced forever on this gift of sea.*
> *An' it harm none, so mote it be.*

In the morning, put the magic love salt in an airtight glass jar and tie a red or pink ribbon round the top. Keep the salt in your magic cupboard - a cupboard or drawer that contains all the ingredients and utensils you would use for magic. This salt can be used exactly as you would any other salt, but be aware that it is infused with the full moon power and the power of St. Valentine's Day for love and all that pertains to it. You could use this salt in your cooking, if making a meal for your intended. You could sprinkle a little around your bedroom if things are getting dull there. You can put it in your bath or make bath salts with it; mix it with rose petals or jasmine oil to create an ambience of amour around you, or to make you desirable to the object of your affection.

There are many traditions and little customs that we can do on Valentine's Day. Of course, we send cards, chocolates and flowers. In certain parts of England gifts would be left on the doorstep and the giver would do his best to escape detection. Similarly when we write a card, traditionally the sender's identity is a secret. Another custom is to put a bay leaf under the pillow on St. Valentine's Eve with the hope of dreaming of one's future husband.

So far we have created a charm of love and created a magic love salt; we have also made a simple but decadent sweet of desire. Here is another generic potion to make, for creating a romantic evening and inducing the feelings of love. You will notice there are nine ingredients, with the quantities of six involved in each. Therefore we are seeking both love and romance with this, and the key ingredient is desire - but also red wine. However, if you do not drink alcohol then use red grape or cherry juice.

Love Potion 69
1 bottle of sweet red wine, or a 1 litre carton of red grape or cherry juice
1 ginseng root cut into 6 equal pieces
6 drops of vanilla extract
6 drops of strawberry juice
6 drops of apple juice
6 basil leaves
6 red rose petals
6 cloves
6 apple seeds

Put all the ingredients together in a saucepan and bring them to the boil. Then reduce the heat and let the mixture simmer for six minutes. Remove it from the heat, strain it through a sieve and allow the potion to cool (it can be drunk warm if you like). Blow six times upon it and bless it in the names of six love goddesses. Then strain it through cheesecloth or a sieve into a clean container such as a wine decanter. Enjoy what happens when you drink it later...

Spells for women seeking men

Here we shall look at the correspondences specifically for women seeking men. The oils to use here are primarily jasmine, red rose, lavender, ylang ylang and bergamot.

Spell One – the love come to me spell
This is a spell for when you want love to come into your heart but have no idea what you are looking for, or what exactly you need. Make a cup of rose tea (from your local health food store). Light a pink candle and sit quietly. While slowly sipping the tea, say these words:

> *Goddess Aphrodite, help me please,*
> *Fill my heart with love.*
> *Show me the one who is meant to be,*
> *Help me find the one I need.*
> *Let him come now, let him come to me.*
> *An' it harm none, so mote it be.*

See what happens in the next couple of days; perhaps you will meet someone or you will realise what it is you are looking for. If not, and you are still undecided after three days, then repeat the spell with the candle and tea for seven nights.

Spell Two – my love's initial spell
This is a spell you can do on a Friday, the day of the goddess Venus. Light a pink candle and pour some of your magic love salt onto a flat service or table big enough to draw a letter in. Ask Venus and Cupid to show you the initial of your true love. Allow the thought to come to you. Then, with eyes closed and

using your index finger, write a letter in the salt. This is your love's initial. Afterwards discard the salt and thank the goddess and her son for their insight.

Spell Three – the true love name spell
Another spell to find the initial of your true love involves peeling a red apple; do it in one long motion so there is plenty of peel. Fill a deep bowl (or the bath) with water and pop a pinch of the magic love salt into it. Then blow on the peel, fill your heart with thoughts of love, and drop it into the water. Watch as the peel opens up to show the initial of your true love.

Charm 1: to charm a necklace
Light one red candle and one pink candle on a Friday night. Take your favourite necklace and recite these words over it:

> *Great messenger, god of love, dear Cupid I ask of you,*
> *Aim your golden arrow and strike this jewellery.*
> *He who notices it will always love me.*
> *An' it harm none, so mote it be.*

Wear the jewellery regularly and if you feel the power wearing off then repeat the charm on a full moon, or sprinkle some magic love salt onto it. The man who notices it first is your intended.

Spell Four – the Mr Right spell
Another spell to summon Mr Right is this: you will need three lit candles forming a triangle. In the space between the candles place an earthen bowl of pink rose petals and three rose quartz stones. Speak the following spell:

> *The perfect man I summon now,*
> *Another way I don't know how.*
> *Bring him now into the light,*
> *Find me please, my Mr Right.*

Oh come to me now, come to me,
An' it harm none, so mote it be.

Spell Five – the healing heart spell
If things have gone a little awry and you are left with a broken heart, you need to restore your strength and faith in love. Carry an ivy leaf in your pocket for strength. Ivy is especially good for women, being a feminine plant. It connects us to the goddess and we are a part of her. Another piece of nature which is perfect for self-love, and after a broken heart, is a little acorn. It can be an actual one or a little silver or gold acorn charm. We are going to call upon the power of the acorn and of nature to restore our bruised faith in love. Remember, from small acorns mighty oak trees grow.

Light three candles - pink, white and green - and place them in a triangle. Say these words:

Father Oak mighty and strong,
My heart is broken by the one.
Love burned and lost, tortured am I,
Help me restore love
Within myself as the weeks go by.
An' it harm none, so mote it be.

Father Oak is another name for the Green Man, the man of the woods, Cerunnos. Call for his strength, but remember always that the power is within you and that you are as sacred as the oak and blessed as the little acorn. Carry the acorn with you wherever you go, keeping it in your bag or purse. Whenever you feel doubt and sadness creeping upon you, take it out and hold it in your hands. Close your eyes and remember the strength of that little acorn, how it grows into a mighty oak.

Spells for women seeking women

Spell-casting of one woman for another woman is different to that of a woman calling for a man. We need different ingredients, as it were. Although some may argue that 'love is love', no, it is not. Different genders have different vibrations and we must learn to blend with those if we want a certain outcome for our spells.

Therefore, the corresponding oils we would use here are myrrh, jasmine, sandalwood, ginger and peach.

The magical Square of the Sun was used in *The Craft in the City*, but there are also other squares that can be used for many different types of spell. Below is the magical Square of Venus; all women can use the Square of Venus spells, but it is particularly potent in woman to woman spells.

22	47	16	41	10	35	4
5	23	48	17	42	11	29
30	6	24	49	18	36	12
13	31	7	25	43	19	37
38	14	32	1	26	44	20
21	39	8	33	2	27	45
46	15	40	9	34	3	28

Spell One – the come to me spell

Use this spell if you know your intended and their name, preferably on a Sunday as we will be using the powers of Venus and the Sun for success and pleasure. Write the name of your beloved on a piece of yellow paper or card and put this on top of the square. Say these words:

> *Goddess Venus, give ... (name)... the strength to come to me.*
> *I know we are meant to be.*
> *Show her the way each and every day.*
> *Come now, come now to me.*
> *An' it harm none, so mote it be.*

Leave the name on the Square of Venus all night and see what happens. Repeat the ritual for fourteen days until your beloved comes.

Spell Two – a spell for enchantment

The Norse goddess Freya is particularly good to call upon in woman to woman spells, though when in doubt always call upon Venus. This enchantment calls specifically upon Freya. Hold a piece of amber or a piece of amber jewellery in your hands and say these words:

> *Goddess Freya,*
> *empower this stone of the north with your charms.*
> *Let the one who looks upon it love me unconditionally.*
> *An' it harm none, so mote it be.*

Hold the amber in your arms for a while, infusing it with energy and power. Wear it, or carry it in your purse, and see who notices you or admires the jewellery.

Spell Three - lily love oil

Lilies and their oil are very sacred. The lily is associated with female spirituality and sensuality. The oil made from the flower was used by ancients for female medical complaints, and Cleopatra was said to use it in her perfume and body oils. We are going to use lilies to create some massage oil for a harmonious atmosphere and a sensual evening.

You will need to buy some essential oils, or make them by the method given in the previous letter, and use a base oil of jasmine or peach oil. Put six drops of lily essential oil, six drops of rose essential oil and six drops of amber oil into the base. It is up to you how much of the base oil you want to use. While you are making the oil say these words:

> *Magic oil, magic oil,*
> *Embrace my love, you and me.*
> *Come to me, sensuality.*
> *Embrace my love, so mote it be.*

After you have made your oil, put it in an airtight bottle and keep it for special, sensual nights with your beloved.

Spell Four – a harmony spell
If there is a bit of tension in your relationship, use this spell. Draw a love heart on a piece of paper and write your name and your loved one's name in the middle of the heart. Recite these words over it as you put six drops of lily essential oil onto it:

> *My love and I have lost sight.*
> *Love is gone and all we do is fight.*
> *Bring us back together.*
> *Let us show love for each other.*
> *Come back to us, respect and harmony.*
> *An' it harm none, so mote it be.*

Then fold the paper up and keep it in a safe place. When the spell has worked, you can burn the paper or simply bury it in the earth, giving thanks to Freya as you do so.

If you can, buy a lily of the valley plant and keep it indoors. The scent is delightful and the little white flowers will bring harmony. However, do not go out and dig up a lily of the valley plant especially. A word of warning: anything growing wild in nature that is white belongs to the goddess. On no account dig it up, pick it or cut it off and bring it indoors, as that will bring bad luck into the house. However, it's fine if something is grown especially for indoors. During the Victorian era, lilies were very popular in houses but now we seem to associate them with funerals for some reason. That's such a shame as they are a beautiful flower of femininity and spirituality. Embrace their magic and let the goddess back into your life.

Spell Five - love forever candle spell
There are many ways to make spells with candles. However, a candle spell is always that much more potent if you have made the candle yourself. The art of candle making is described in detail in *The Craft in the City*.

Make a peach-coloured candle, within which put three drops each of myrrh, jasmine and sandalwood essential oils. If you do not want to make the candle, then anoint a bought peach-coloured candle with these oils. As you do so, say these words:

> *Candle magic, candle flame,*
> *Enlighten love.*
> *My beloved I shall name.*
> *Let ...(name)... and I be of one heart*
> *For now and evermore.*
> *An' it harm none, so mote it be.*

This is a rather potent spell, so be sure that you want to be with the one you are with for now and evermore. Spells can turn out in ways we would never have imagined, so be careful what you cast for!

Spells for men seeking women

The correspondences used in this section are different again. This time the man is doing all the hard work by drawing the woman to him. Here it is Mars and Venus, the ultimate lovers, whom we call upon. However, there are several couples we could use here as gods and goddesses: Jupiter and Juno, Neptune and Minerva, Apollo and Diana or Vulcan and Vesta.

Here it is male energy seeking out female energy. So the oil correspondences to use are gardenia, geranium, rose, jojoba oil base, lavender and grape, and the colours to be used are predominately reds.

Each of the gods and goddesses has their own colour too:

Zeus, Jupiter, Odin – white, silver
Poseidon, Neptune – blue
Ares, Mars, Thor – red
Aphrodite, Venus – pink
Hera, Juno – gold
Demeter, Gaia – green
Hades, Orcus, Pluto, Hecate – black
Athena, Minerva, Freya – yellow

Spell One - come to me candle spell
Buy a red candle and anoint it with rose, lavender and jojoba oil. If you can make the candle yourself, put three drops each of these oils into the red candle and wait for it to set. Now place a needle halfway into the candle. As you push the needle in, envision the woman of your dreams, or the one you've met, coming to you.

Light the candle and as you do so, say these words:

> *Love, love, come to me.*
> *Love, love, and set my passion free.*
> *An' it harm none, so mote it be.*

The spell will take effect when the flame reaches the needle, and the woman you want will feel the pull to you.

Spell Two - send my love to me spell
Buy a rose, geranium, gardenia or lavender plant and keep it indoors or outdoors, whichever is best for the plant. But understand that this plant is a gift to the goddess Venus for helping you in your spell. Write the name of your beloved either in red or on red paper or card and fold this six times. Then put the folded paper or card into the soil with the plant, and say these words:

> *Venus and Mars, lovers of old,*
> *Send my love to me, let love unfold.*
> *This name I give to show thee.*
> *This plant I give to you.*
> *Let its flowers bloom with love*
> *As my love flourishes.*
> *An' it harm none, so mote it be.*

Lovingly nurture the plant, either indoors or out in the garden. As the plant grows, so will the love between you and your beloved.

Spell Three - Aphrodite love apple spell for happy union
There are many famous stories in both Greek and Norse mythology concerning the apple. For us, the apple is a constant reminder that magic and the goddess are always with us. Cut an apple in half and you will find the pentagram, our most sacred symbol.

In this spell you are going to create a charm for a happy union, a marriage or relationship. Take a red apple and slice it across, creating very thin slices that have the pentagram within them. Leave these slices in the open air for a while until they have withered and look a bit like leather. If you have magic love salt then use it here, but if not then sea salt will do (after all, Aphrodite came from the sea). Sprinkle the salt over the withered pieces of apple, saying these words:

> *Aphrodite, goddess of love*
> *Grant your blessings upon this fruit.*
> *Bless me always in matrimony.*
> *Let my marriage to ...(name)...*
> *Be full of love and always be happy.*
> *An' it harm none, so mote it be.*

Give one of your slices to your partner and keep one for yourself. Keep it in your wallet, and hers in her purse. Whenever you feel the need to recharge the love between you both, hold the apple slice in your hands and remember the love you feel for one another.

Spell Four – the king and queen healing spell

Here is a very old and exquisite spell. You will need the king and queen chess pieces. They can be either black or white, or both the same colour; it is just the genders that are important. This is a good spell if you are having trouble in the relationship and no-one is communicating very well. Place the king at one end of a shelf, a mantelpiece or even a room. Place the queen in the opposite direction, so the king is at one end and the queen is at the other. Say these words:

> *Bring together my love and me,*
> *For now and evermore.*
> *An' it harm none, so mote it be.*

Each day, bring the two chess pieces a little closer until finally they are almost touching one another. The spell is now complete and you and your beloved should be closer together.

Spell Five - Celtic chestnut love spell
There are many spells involving chestnuts, or conkers as we call them in the UK. Chestnuts were used in many Celtic love spells, though ironically the horse chestnut tree is not native to the British Isles but to the forests and mountain areas of southeast Europe. Nevertheless it has found its way into our culture and spells.

The intent of this spell is to keep the love alive. Make a hole through each of three chestnuts and tie them together with red cord or ribbon, with three knots in between each chestnut. Then light a red candle and say:

> *Lord and lady of light and dark,*
> *Grant love for evermore to my partner and me.*
> *To couples everywhere, blessed be.*
> *An' it harm none, so mote it be.*

Keep the chestnut charm in a safe place for a year, then you can bury it in a garden, giving thanks to the lord and lady.

Spells for men seeking men

Once again the correspondences are different to those used earlier, for spells that involve a man seeking another man need to channel the male energies of magic. The corresponding oils to be used are cinnamon, sweet almond oil, vanilla, sandalwood, sage, cypress, musk and patchouli. The gods to be addressed are Mars, who has pure male energy and will be employed in most of our spells, but also Thor and Eros; and also let us return to the beginning and bring Cupid to our aid. The colours we should use are white, red, magnolia, green and black.

We shall also use the Square of Mars. This is an 'eleven' square. Each line counted either horizontally, vertically or diagonally adds up to sixty-five, which breaks down to 6 + 5 = 11. Eleven is itself a very magical and sacred number that personifies intuition and idealism. However, I would reduce this number down to its single form, which of course is 1 + 1 = 2. When it comes to love, two is a beautiful number; two people in a relationship, two souls. The number two also represents empathy and co-operation, which are important in any relationship.

The Square of Mars

11	24	7	20	3
4	12	25	8	16
17	5	13	21	9
10	18	1	14	22
23	6	19	2	15

Spell One – a come to me spell

It is the candle and needle spell described earlier, with a little extra. Make a white candle and into it put three drops each of sandalwood, musk and patchouli oils. If instead you choose to buy a white candle, anoint it with these oils. Then score the name of your beloved into the candle. Push a needle halfway into the candle and say these words:

> *This candle I shall claim.*
> *May the love for my beloved*
> *Burn as strong as the flame.*
> *Scored within my heart forever his name.*
> *Let him know how much I feel.*
> *Let him feel all that I feel.*
> *Let us share in the love, blessed be.*
> *An' it harm none, so mote it be.*

When the flame burns down to the needle, the spell begins to take effect. You can use this spell again and again, moving the needle down further each time until the candle is no more (always move the needle when the flame is not lit) although you may only need to do this spell once.

Spell Two - male magic Mars salt

If a full moon falls on a Tuesday, the day of Mars, then we can use the Square of Mars. Write out the Square of Mars on a piece of red card and place a bowl filled with sea salt on top of it, in view of the full moon. As you do so, say these words:

> *Hear me Diana, hear me Mars,*
> *Bestow your fortunes upon this gift of sea.*
> *Let love, passion and honour flow to me.*
> *An' it harm none, so mote it be.*

Leave the bowl in view of the moon all night and in the morning put the salt into an airtight glass jar. Tie a red ribbon round it. This magic Mars salt is for anything that needs some extra energy. You can use it in cooking, in your bath, or even in candle-making; one pinch is all that's needed. Remember, it has been graced by the god Mars, a god of pure male energy, power, passion and action. So use it wisely!

Spell Three - cinnamon sizzle spell

If things have got a little boring in the bedroom, then pop two drops of cinnamon oil in the soap dispenser of your washing machine when washing your bedding. Say these words as you do so:

> *Sizzle me cinnamon,*
> *Sizzle me quick.*
> *Let love and passion come to me.*
> *An' it harm none, so mote it be.*

Wash and dry the sheets as normal, and enjoy...

Spell Four – a sensual sex spell

Here we are going to make some 'Triple S' massage oil especially for men. The base oil to use is sweet almond. Put three drops each of cinnamon, musk and sandalwood essential oils into the base oil. It is up to you how much base oil you use. Say these words as you shake up the oil:

> *Three times three,*
> *Eros I call to thee.*
> *Grant pleasure to my love and me.*
> *An' it harm none, so mote it be.*

After you have made the Triple S oil, put it into a dark glass bottle and date it.

Spell Five – the 'What's it all about?' spell
If there is some distance in your relationship and you don't know what has happened or where it has gone wrong, this spell is right for you. It asks Cupid to bring you back together again as a couple. This spell also helps your partner to tell you what's wrong. Use a white candle. If you have made the candle, put three drops each of sage, cypress and vanilla essential oils into it. If it's a bought candle then anoint it with these oils. Light the candle and say these words:

> *Cupid, I beseech thee,*
> *Bring my love closer to me.*
> *Our love is strong*
> *But now there is something wrong.*
> *Let ...(name)... speak to me*
> *Of our wrongs and pain,*
> *So that we may love again.*
> *An' it harm none, so mote it be.*

You could prepare a meal of asparagus, mushrooms and stuffed red peppers with rosemary, or if not vegetarian then a chicken and rosemary dinner. Then allow your partner to talk to you over dinner, while the candle is alight on the table, and see how the evening develops.

There you have it, twenty spells on love and hardly a rose petal among them! There are many other spells that could have been put into this letter, such as spells for fertility, but these can be found in the Family letter of this book. The next few pages also list some other herbs, fruits, crystals and oils that may be used in love spells.

There is one last thing to be said here regarding love and that concerns marriage. In the Craft we have no bias; love is in the eye of the beholder, no matter which gender it falls upon. Therefore, in our tradition marriage is referred to as hand fasting, which means one soul being bound to another in this life and the next. It is not a ceremony to be taken lightly. The full ceremony, and a description of hand fasting, can be found in *The Witch in the City*, along with many other life festivals and ceremonies.

Blessed Be

More Love Spell Ingredients

Herbs and Fruit

Apples are used in spells for love and for healing. The core of the fruit is a natural pentagram.

Cardamom can also be used for spells of love and lust.

Cumin is a herb that has been used for centuries by women as an aid to conception.

Fenugreek is a herb with the delightful nickname of 'the breast enhancer.' It was often given to women in harems. You can still get it in herbal food shops, in pill or tea form.

Lavender is one of the most popular ingredients in love spells. The fragrant plant is also often used by midwives to ease childbirth.

Liverwort is used in spells for love and protection.

Mandrake is believed to be the most magical of all herbs. The mandrake root is the most powerful herb in love magic - as well as one of the deadliest, so take care.

Rosemary is a herb of love enchantment and can be used in spells provoking lust.

Crystals

Clear Quartz is the master healing crystal but it also brings balance, harmony and love. This is a crystal that can be used particularly for male love spells.

Magnetite is a dark, granular-looking stone formed from iron and, because it is magnetic, it is regarded as the ideal stone for attracting love and developing a balanced relationship. Male to male spells and charms are also improved when using this stone.

Rose Quartz is the stone of unconditional love. It also opens the heart chakra (or energy centre).

Rhodochrosite is a stone that attracts love.

Soul mate crystal – this is two clear crystals of similar size growing from a common base. Place it in the furthest right-hand corner from the door in your bedroom.

Oils

Aniseed oil was used by the ancients for massage. It is good for male spells.

Cinnamon oil has been used as an aphrodisiac. The oil was sprinkled over beds for a good, energetic night.

Lotus oil is used as an aphrodisiac. If you can get your hands on some, it's definitely worth it!

Money

Dear Reader,

This is the topic people ask witches about most often, second only to love. Here there are many spells to cover all different areas associated with money, including debt, credit, savings, investments and dealing with people who owe you money, to mention just a few. So let us take a close look at this massive topic and see what correspondences we need to use.

The gods and goddesses of wealth and money are usually responsible for more than one area. For example, one of the key goddesses in money spells is the Celtic-Roman goddess Rosmerta, the consort of the god Mercury. She is also the goddess of fertility and abundance. In ancient depictions of her she is usually holding a purse, which is why she was often called upon to help with money issues. Mercury himself is the Roman god of financial gain, commerce, communication and luck, among other things, so he is a very valuable god to be aware of when dealing with money matters. The other gods and goddesses for money and wealth are Juno, Abundantia, Hermes and Plutus (not to be confused with Pluto, also a god of wealth). Finally we have Cerunnos who was a god of wealth and in Norse religion the Viking Njord was a very wealthy god who granted land and wealth to worthy people, so he's one worth remembering too.

The colours to be used in wealth spells are green, silver, gold and yellow. The oils and herbs to use are saffron, mint, ginger, basil, nutmeg, lemon balm, honeysuckle, cinnamon, marjoram and bay.

As with all things magical, money spells may require us to change our attitudes towards wealth. For example, we need to shift our thinking from 'make do' to 'I deserve more'. But then the universe can only do so much - we have to do some work too. We should start by sorting out our finances, checking statements and commitments - do you need that gym membership when you've only been once in six months? The next twenty spells on money and areas related to it are ways of channelling your thoughts and your will towards getting the outcome you desire.

And by the way, we never mention to others that we have done a money spell. When working with money magic, we keep quiet until it has taken effect (if we ever do tell people at all about our spell work).

Here is a lovely little money potion. However, it only lasts for fourteen days so make sure you date the jar.

Spell One – a money potion spell
1 tsp cinnamon
1 tsp ground bay leaves
1 tsp basil
1 tsp marjoram

Grind the ingredients together with a pestle and mortar, and while doing so say these words:

> *Money, money, money,*
> *Come to me.*
> *An' it harm none, so mote it be.*

Stir four times and put the potion in a jar with a tight lid (such as a washed and dried, empty coffee jar). Keep the jar near your finances, for example your bank book or credit cards, but remember only to keep it for fourteen days.

You will have noticed that this potion requires one teaspoon each of the four ingredients and it is stirred four times.

The number four relates to material matters, wealth and communication. The number eight is also a very auspicious number regarding financial concerns. Therefore many of the spells here regarding money will have the quantities of four or eight in them.

Spell Two – the green apple spell
The apple is our friend and one of the main fruits we can use for almost any magical work, because the apple holds within its heart the pentagram. In love spells we use a red apple, but for money spells we use a green one.

Slice one green apple very thinly across so that the pentagram is in each slice. Draw the pentagram on a piece of green paper, or on white paper with a green pen. Leave the apple slices for a couple of days to completely dry out. They should look and feel a bit like leather. Light a green candle. Place four apple slices on the pentagram, leaving the top point empty as that represents spirit, or the divine.[3] Say these words:

> *Green apple offerings of pentagram might*
> *Help my purse be not so light.*
> *Dear goddess Juno, lady of commerce,*
> *Bestow your gifts of financial plenty upon these offerings.*
> *May they bring prosperity in the purse they belong to.*
> *An' it harm none, so mote it be.*

Keep the candle burning as long as possible. Focus your thoughts on money coming into your life like the rays of light coming from the candle. Afterwards, keep one of the apple slices in your purse. You could give the other three to friends who may have need of them, to keep in their wallets or purses.

---

[3] Detailed information about the pentagram, and how to draw it, is given in *The Witch in the City*.

Spell Three – the 'Venus help me' spell

Write out the Square of Venus (see the letter on love spells) on green card or paper. Do this spell on a Friday night. We are going to ask the goddess Venus for some financial help. Write the amount of money you need on a piece of paper and put it on top of the Square of Venus. Say these words as you do so:

> *Goddess Venus, help me please.*
> *This amount of money I need.*
> *Blessed Venus, thank you for your gifts.*
> *An' it harm none, so mote it be.*

Leave the paper on the Square of Venus all night and in the morning fold it four times and place it in a drawer. If nothing happens in about a week, do this ritual again for seven nights.

The Square of Venus is very good for money spells. If you add up all the numbers horizontally, vertically or diagonally, they add up to 175. Breaking this number down to 1 + 7 + 5 we get 13, and 1 + 3 is 4, the number of money and wealth. That is precisely what spell casting is about, weaving through connections, the elements, space and time in order to achieve the goal we desire.

Spell Four – a money candle spell

If you can make a green candle, put a drop each of mint, basil, bay and cinnamon essential oils into it and allow it to set. If you buy your green candle, anoint it with the oils mentioned. Put a needle halfway into the candle and as you do so imagine the amount of money you need coming to you. Then light the candle and say these words:

> *Money, money, come to me.*
> *Burning flame, let it be.*
> *An' it harm none, so mote it be.*

The spell takes effect when the flame reaches the needle.

Spell Five – the cheque it out spell
This is a very easy spell to do. If you have a cheque book, fill out a blank cheque with the amount of money you desire. Put one drop each of basil, mint, saffron and marjoram essential oils onto the cheque and fold it into four. While folding, say these words:

> *North, south, east, west,*
> *Four quarters I implore*
> *Grant me the money I ask for.*
> *Let the money flow to me.*
> *An' it harm none, so mote it be.*

Put the folded cheque in your purse or wallet until the money comes to you.

Spell Six – the send me the money spell
If someone owes you money but is not paying up, then try this spell. On a piece of yellow card or paper, write their name and how much is owed to you. Draw the pentagram on the paper too. Then hold the paper in your hands as you say:

> *Mighty and powerful Mercury,*
> *Bring money and justice to me.*
> *Let all that I am owed come back to me.*
> *An' it harm none, so mote it be.*

Fold the paper into four and keep it with your financial information.

Spell Seven – a nest egg spell
If you are trying to save for something in particular but every month something seems to happen, leaving you without anything to save, then this spell is for you.

There are many spells involving eggs, from fertility to protection spells, but this one is particularly good for those trying to save. Make two holes in an egg, one at the top and one below, then blow out the yolk etcetera. It can take a while and you may need several attempts at it. If you prefer, you can put a small straw in the hole at the top and then blow out the egg that way.

When you have blown out the egg, wash it by running cool water through it and leave it to dry. Write on a small piece of paper how much you want your savings to grow: £1,000, £10,000…? It is entirely up to you how much you would like.

When your egg is completely dry, roll up the paper and place it carefully inside the egg. If you have a garden, bury the egg outdoors. If not, see if you can buy a money plant and bury the egg in the soil near the plant. As you bury it, say these words:

> *Little nest egg, grow for me.*
> *Big and strong you shall be.*
> *All my savings shall grow with money.*
> *An' it harm none, so mote it be.*

Lovingly tend to the plant and watch your nest egg grow.

Spell Eight – a credit card spell

This spell requires you to shift your consciousness. If you wish to be free of debt and owing money on your credit cards, then try this spell. Place all your credit or store cards in a bowl. Next take a pair of scissors and cut all but one of them up! (If they are all maxed out then cut every one of them up.) You do not need them and you are trying to be debt free. Cut each card into four pieces and while doing so say these words:

> *In months of three*
> *I will be debt free.*
> *These cards I do not need.*
> *I cut up and release them.*
> *Mighty Mercury, show me the way*

> *To clear these cards with full pay.*
> *Mighty Mercury, thank you and blessed be.*
> *An' it harm none, so mote it be.*

Set your mind to pay the cards off in three months, or you can rewrite the spell depending on how many cards you have. Just make sure the spell has eight lines, as we need the power of eight with this one.

Think of different ways to save money. Sort out things you no longer need or want, such as jewellery, clothes and presents that have never been opened. Sell items that are no longer needed. For example, have a car boot sale or hire a stall at your local market one weekend, and offload everything to get the money you need to pay off the cards with.

Spell Nine – the acorn increase prosperity spell

Acorns are not just good for attracting a lover, they also increase income and prosperity. If you can, find a real acorn and spray it with gold paint (better still to collect several and spray them all gold). When they are dry, put them in the shape of a pentagram, or draw the pentagram on a piece of yellow card or paper. You will also need some gold material, cut into five circles the size of a saucer, and some green ribbon; we are going to make little pouches with them.

Put an acorn on each of the five points of the pentagram and if you have more then put them in the centre of the pentagram. If you just have one then put that in the centre. Sprinkle some saffron over the golden acorns. Light a yellow candle and say these words:

> *Money flow to me from every point,*
> *North, south, east, west.*
> *Money come to me which way seems best.*
> *Please pentagram magic, blessed be.*
> *An' it harm none, so mote it be.*

Say the rhyme five times and each time imagine money coming to you from each of the points of the pentagram, like the beams of lights streaking out from the candle.

Afterwards, put an acorn in the centre of each gold circle of material, gather it up and tie it with the green ribbon. If you only have one acorn, that's fine; keep the gold bag near to your bank details or where you keep money. If you have five acorns, then put the gold pouches around your house or in the corners of your rooms. You can hang them up, or hide them if you haven't yet ventured out of the broom cupboard and don't want to have to explain anything to nosey people.

Spell Ten - the money jar spell
This is similar to the golden acorn spell but instead it uses a jar, and you consciously add money each week. You will need a clean, empty jam jar or similar, a pen and paper, four coins of the highest denomination you can afford, one bay leaf and two pinches of saffron.

On the bay leaf, write your name. On the paper, write what you want the money for, for example a car, a holiday, your college fund etcetera. Then fold the paper up four times. Put the folded paper in the jar followed by the bay leaf. Next put the coins in one at a time and as you do so imagine each coin multiplying ten times. After you have the coins in, put the pinches of saffron into the jar. Afterwards, put the lid on the jar and hold it in your hands as you say:

> *Goddess Rosmerta, abundance be,*
> *Help the coins grow for me.*
> *Money magic of Rosmerta bright,*
> *Grow forever more with such might.*
> *An' it harm none, so mote it be.*

Keep the jar in a place that you can see all the time, though once again not in view of anyone else. Every four days, try to put another coin in the jar until it is full or until you have what is written on the paper. When you do have what you want, empty the jar and bury the bay leaf and paper in the garden, giving thanks to Rosmerta as you do so. If you do not have a garden, then burn them and sprinkle salt over the remains, which you can then throw away. Wash the jar and keep it for use in other magical work.

Spell Eleven – the leprechaun money magic spell
Gold is revered today as much as it was in the ancient world. Gold is magical and powerful, and was the object of kings and gods. It is the colour of the sun and with it comes the power of the sun. There were many magical beings whose responsibility was the protection and ownership of gold. Here in this spell we are going to channel some leprechaun magic. These peculiar little folk of Ireland were fine craftsmen of shoes and knew a thing or two about making and saving money. They hid their pots of gold at the ends of rainbows, although to them gold was not just shiny wealth but was also regarded as magic in its purest form.

You may not believe that leprechauns exist, but it is what they represent that matters to us here - wealth and magic, and we want both. You will need one green candle, four gold coins (such as £1 coins), some gold material cut into a circle the size of a small plate, and some black ribbon. The ribbon represents the actual pot the leprechauns kept their gold in, which was usually black.

Light the green candle and place the four coins around it, saying these words:

> *Golden magic of leprechaun charm,*
> *An' it do no harm,*
> *Magic pot of gold,*
> *Send me the wealth of old.*
> *Golden magic, send wealth to me.*
> *Leprechaun magic, so mote it be.*

Afterwards, meditate on the flame. Imagine your own pot of gold overflowing with money. Then put the coins in the centre of the circle of gold material and secure it with the black ribbon, like a pouch. Keep the gold bundle in a place where you keep your financial papers, and let the candle burn down by itself.

Spell Twelve - the star sign money spell
Here we are going to channel the energies of our own individual star sign. Each sign has a special lucky day associated with it so let us use this and do the money spell on your personal day. Here is a list of the star signs and their lucky days:

Aries – Tuesday	Leo – Sunday	Sagittarius - Thursday
Taurus – Friday	Virgo – Wednesday	Capricorn - Saturday
Gemini – Wednesday	Libra – Friday	Aquarius - Saturday
Cancer – Monday	Scorpio – Tuesday	Pisces – Thursday

On your personal star sign day, light a green candle that has been anointed with basil, bay, mint and marjoram oils. Say these words:

> *Star light, star bright,*
> *Please send your money might.*
> *Bestow the riches of the universe on me.*
> *An' it harm none, so mote it be.*

Let the candle burn itself out, or try to keep it burning as long as possible (though never leave a burning candle unattended).

Spell Thirteen – a money charm spell
2 cinnamon sticks
2 bay leaves
Some thin green ribbon

Do this spell on a Friday night. Make a hole in the bay leaves, small enough to let the thin green ribbon go through. Tie the cinnamon sticks together with the ribbon. Thread the ribbon through the bay leaves so that the cinnamon sticks and bay leaves are together, and secure them with a bow. As you make the charm, say these words:

> *Goddess Venus, blessed be.*
> *Send your financial wisdom to me.*
> *Goddess Venus, I beseech thee*
> *Please send money to me.*
> *An' it harm none, so mote it be.*

Hang the charm somewhere in sight, such as the kitchen or the room you use most. Indeed, you could make several of them and put them in every room of the house. They also make nice gifts for friends. You could make up a money basket for a friend, with the money charm, a green candle and a golden acorn. It's always good to think of others when working with money magic.

Spell Fourteen – the dragon gold spell
Legend tells us that dragons loved two things, virgins and gold! They loved gold as much as any king or god and would hoard it in great caves; woe betide the brave but annoying knight who ventured near enough to steal it.

Do this spell on any day you wish except April 23rd, St George's Day. We must, after all, try to respect the poor dragons. Burn a red candle and have a piece of obsidian, which by some people is still called 'dragon stone' as it was forged in volcanoes. Another dragon stone is septarain, which has the appearance of scales. With the obsidian or septarain near the candle, say these words:

> *Mighty dragons, lovers of gold,*
> *Your strength and powers of old*

> *Help me in my quest.*
> *Fill me with your power and zest.*
> *Grant the wealth of your yellow metal,*
> *Sweep through the centuries to me.*
> *An' it harm none, so mote it be.*

If the flame flickers they have heard your request; do not be frightened, just embrace their magic. Keep the piece of obsidian or septarain in your purse or wallet.

Spell Fifteen – a goldstone charm
This is a good spell if you have a meeting with a bank manager or an accountant, or anyone who might be able to grant you money, such as a mortgage or a loan. It is good for any meeting with someone connected with finances and money. You want some money luck to rub off on you.

See if you can find a goldstone bracelet or necklace, any piece of goldstone jewellery that you can wear every day. Light a gold or yellow candle. If you make it yourself it needs four pinches of saffron in it; if it is bought then anoint it with saffron oil. Place the goldstone jewellery around or near the candle and say these words:

> *My finances have run amok.*
> *Goddess Juno, send me money luck.*
> *Place upon this stone of gold.*
> *Let my finances increase tenfold.*
> *Goddess Juno, thank you and blessed be.*
> *An' it harm none, so mote it be.*

Let the candle burn as long as you can, then extinguish it (but do not blow it out). Wear the goldstone jewellery whenever you have an important financial meeting.

Spell Sixteen – the 'return to me' spell

Here is another spell for when someone is holding on to your money. We are going to ask Pluto to help. Pluto is a rather formidable god and a force to be reckoned with!

You will need a black candle and a green candle. Please do this spell in a circle of salt: just sprinkle some salt around you and make sure that you have all you need already in the circle before you begin. Say this:

> *Mighty Pluto, truth and justice I seek.*
> *Another owes me money.*
> *Their name is ...(name)...*
> *Let their conscience be pricked,*
> *Let what is rightfully mine return to me.*
> *An' it harm none, mighty Pluto, so mote it be.*

Say the spell four times over the burning candles. Afterwards, give thanks to Pluto and extinguish the candles with a candle snuffer. Do not blow out these candles.

Wait a week and see what happens; if the person withholding your money has not been in touch, then perform the spell again but only do this a maximum of three times. You do not want to annoy Pluto – after all, he is the god of the Underworld!

Spell Seventeen – the 'help me save money' spell

If you would like to save money but are always overdrawn by the end of the month, then this spell is for you. Anoint a silver candle with basil oil, light it and say these words:

> *Universe, help me to save.*
> *Help me to put money away.*
> *Help me to save for a rainy day.*
> *Help me to have some money for me.*
> *An' it harm none, so mote it be.*

Do the spell for eight nights. Write out a saving plan for the next four months!

Spell Eighteen – a money guidance spell
If you have absolutely no idea what to do regarding money, then ask the gods for help and guidance in trying to fathom out your finances. Try to do this spell on a Wednesday, lighting a silver candle and reciting these words:

> *Mighty Hermes, your guidance I need.*
> *My money and finances are a mess.*
> *The best course of action I know not.*
> *Please Hermes, show me the way,*
> *The best paths to take for my pay.*
> *Thank you Hermes, and blessed be.*
> *An' it harm none, so mote it be.*

When you go to sleep at night, have a pen and paper handy as the answer may come to you in a dream. But it could be at any time, so carry a pen and paper with you always. Repeat the spell for seven nights until you have an answer. When you do, thank Hermes.

Spell Nineteen – the 'end my money woes' spell
Use a green candle and have some basil seeds nearby. We are going to plant the basil seeds and watch your money grow. Recite this over the green candle:

> *Help me, Cerunnos,*
> *Save me from my money woes.*
> *Shed light on my financial strife*
> *To help me find the path that is right.*
> *Great Cerunnos, blessed be.*
> *An' it harm none, so mote it be.*

Plant the seeds in a little pot of soil and tenderly care for them.

Ask Cerunnos for help with money woes often, so that they become less and less.

Spell Twenty - the gods of the north money spell
In this spell we are going to ask the Norse god Njord for help in receiving wealth. He is the god of the sea, of wind, fishing, wealth and fertility, so he really is a useful god to be aware of. Find a piece of amber, often known as 'the gold of the north'. Light a yellow candle and place the amber in view of the flame, saying:

> *Great Njord, bestow your gifts,*
> *Your strength, your money power to me.*
> *Bless this gold of the north with riches galore.*
> *An' it harm none, so mote it be.*

Put the piece of amber in your purse or wallet. For this spell, it is all right to blow out the candle as Njord is also the god of the wind. Imagine the candle smoke rising through the winds to Njord, whispering your plea to him.

So here are twenty money spells for all different financial occasions and situations. Use them wisely and, remember, do not speak of your money magic dealings to others until the spells have done their work.

You can of course change the wording of any spell to suit your own particular situation. In the next letter, we shall look at the subject of careers, which can also be related to financial rewards.

Blessed Be

More Money Correspondences

Herbs and Fruit

Allspice is a good spice for money and wealth spells (and for healing). It makes a good incense.

Anise hyssop leaves have anti-bacterial properties and also make a refreshing tea with a minty flavour.

Cinnamon has so many wondrous uses, it is a staple basic in any witch's kitchen.

Cloves are wonderful, but do not put the actual cloves into candles as they can ignite and combust. If you would like to put the scent into a candle, then use the oil instead.

Pomegranate is a great fruit for fertility and for money.

Thyme is an antiseptic, anti-bacterial and anti-fungal herb. It is a truly wonderful plant for anything and everything, though not to be used during pregnancy as it is a uterine stimulant.

Crystals

Citrine has always been a great stone throughout history. In many countries, merchants would carry a piece in their money boxes, thus it became known as the Merchant's Stone.

Emerald is great for legal or business matters, so carry a piece when next seeing the bank manager.

Peridot is a good stone for helping you decide your destiny.

Sapphire is the stone of wisdom, loyalty and truth.

Turquoise is the traveller's stone.

Essential Oils

Honeysuckle is a beautifully smelling oil, very sensual but also very positive when used in money spells.

Nutmeg oil should always be used sparingly as it does have a toxic compound which can cause hallucinations and convulsions - please be careful with this.

Oak moss oil blends well with orange oil and can be used as an antiseptic.

Saffron oil is fantastic for its digestive properties; it also improves circulation and reduces high blood pressure. It is the richest known source of Vitamin B2.

Career

Dear Reader,

This subject covers many areas from promotion and job success to finding the right job. There are many gods and goddesses to call upon for help. The goddess Lakshmi is one to turn to, as is Athena, the goddess of wisdom. Artemis, or Diana, is the goddess of the hunt, while the goddess Brighid can also be asked for inspiration with creative pursuits. And as always, the goddess Juno never fails to help even though she is more associated with money, motherhood and matrimony.

The gods we can ask are Jupiter, Mars, Mercury, Apollo and Zeus. Moreover, depending on the type of work you do, each vocational area has a designated god or goddess attached to it. For example, Athena is the goddess of teachers and those who work in education.

The colour correspondences used in career spells are often yellow, orange, silver and red. The herbs are bergamot, dill, lemongrass, jasmine, fennel and tarragon, while the oils are pine, rosemary, frankincense and sandalwood. The number I shall use here is three, as it is the number of sociability - we do need to get along with others in our work. It is also the number of artistic expression and all of us, no matter how mundane our jobs, can find some creativity in them.

Spell One - career clarity spell

This is a spell to clarify which direction you should follow for satisfaction in your work. Light a yellow candle anointed with frankincense and sandalwood oils. Say these words:

> *My life is hard, decisions abound.*
> *Show me the way that I can see,*
> *Help me to know clarity.*
> *Wheel of life round and round,*
> *Am I up or am I down?*
> *So much strife in work have I,*
> *No balance, no life, constant fight.*
> *Please Mother Juno, help,*
> *Guide me to restore balance,*
> *Let me be strong to take a chance.*
> *An' it harm none, so mote it be.*

Keep a pen and paper with you or better still your own Book of Shadows. The answer to your career clarity will be shown to you within the next month. Look for the signs; they may appear in different forms, but trust your instincts. You will know what is right and wrong in your working life, and how to resolve it.

Spell Two – the always late spell

This is a good spell if you are always late despite your best intentions. For this a silver candle is needed, with a piece of citrine. Have the candle lit and let the citrine pass through the flames three times. Say these words as you move the citrine just above the flame:

> *In the morning I am always late.*
> *The bus with people cannot wait.*
> *Help time to stand still*
> *So that I can do the day's fill.*
> *An' it harm none, so mote it be.*

Keep the citrine with you at all times, in your purse, wallet or college bag, or whatever you take with you when you are constantly late.

Spell Three – the CV blast spell
When you know the job you want, you just need to get it. You need a CV that will make bosses hire you on the spot. So research the most up to date CVs on the Internet and spend twenty-four hours working on yours. While you do so, recite these words:

> *I work on my CV for twenty-four hours.*
> *Grant me success and power.*
> *Above the rest will be my CV.*
> *An' it harm none, so mote it be.*

After you have completed the spell and written your CV, put it in a drawer for twenty-four hours and forget about it. Then take it out and look at it again. Trust your instincts about any changes that need to be made, until you are ready to send it away to your prospective employers.

Spell Four - the Ofsted spell
This is a spell specially written for any educational establishment that has a visit from the government inspectors.

Light three good luck incense cones, or three pine incense sticks. You also need five horse chestnuts arranged in the shape of the pentagram as you recite this spell:

> *Goddess Athena, hear my request,*
> *Help ...(name)... to be the best*
> *In their inspection by Ofsted.*
> *Help the staff to be outstanding.*
> *To one and all, blessed be.*
> *An' it harm none, so mote it be.*

In spells like this you could also include the days on which the inspectors will visit. As always with spell-weaving, it helps to be specific.

Spell Five – a forgiveness at work spell
Sometimes in our place of work we encounter enemies whom we need to forgive in order to move on. Although it is often difficult to forget things, we can always try to forgive and go forward in the knowledge that we tried.

For this spell we need frankincense and rosemary oils in a red candle, if made yourself. If bought, anoint it with these oils. Write the name of the person you need to forgive on a piece of red paper. Light the candle and focus on the name as you say these words:

> *Universe, hear my plea.*
> *From anger towards ...(name)... I am free.*
> *Let me forgive ...(name)...*
> *For all the pain they sent me.*
> *An' it harm none, so mote it be.*

Afterwards, burn the paper and wash the burnt pieces away with salt water. You might do this spell near the sink so you can just wash everything away. Remember, though, to keep the candle away from the water!

Spell Six – a gossip mongers spell
At times, no matter how well we do at work, there are always those who spread vicious gossip. The children's rhyme, 'Sticks and stones may hurt my bones but words can never break me' is often quoted. However, words do hurt and they can even be more damaging than sticks and stones. This is a spell, basically, to send it all back to the gossip mongers.

If possible, have a snapdragon flower or plant. If you cannot get hold of one then a picture will suffice, but the real thing is best. As with herbs, dried ones are fine but the fresher the better! You also need a mirror, a red pen or red paper and a tiger's eye. This is a wonderful crystal and perfect for this occasion because it makes those who spread vicious lies think twice; and with the added kick of the mirror we are going to send it right back to them.

In the light of an orange candle, place the snapdragon next to the tiger's eye. Write the culprit's name on a piece of paper; either the pen or the paper needs to be red. Stand the mirror behind the flame so that you can see your own face as well as the snapdragon and tiger's eye reflected in it. Say these words:

> *Your words of hatred I send back to thee.*
> *Your thoughts and lies of deceit I return to thee.*
> *...(name)... no longer shall you give pain,*
> *For I shall send it back to you again and again.*
> *Snapdragon and tiger's eye will end your deceitful lies.*
> *But no harm will come to anyone, for all blessed be.*
> *For now and ever more, so mote it be.*

Afterwards, keep the candle burning for as long as possible before extinguishing it properly. Keep the name, snapdragon and mirror in view or on your altar for the next seven days. Take the tiger's eye with you to work and keep it with you at all times (or in your desk). After seven days, bury the snapdragon and paper in the garden if possible. If you do not have a garden, then burn the paper and dispose of everything in the usual way.

Spell Seven – a new moon new job spell
Suppose you now have a nice new job - well done. Write down your goals for the new job, both personal and professional. Decide ten goals or targets for the coming year (or for however long the contract lasts). Make a yellow candle with lemongrass and bergamot in it, or anoint a bought yellow candle with

these oils. On a night of the new moon, light the candle; then holding your ten goals in your hand, say these words:

> *Father Jupiter, blessed be,*
> *A new job have I.*
> *Grant me success in goals of ten,*
> *Help me prove my worth and then*
> *Victorious I shall be.*
> *An' it harm none, so mote it be.*

Meditate on your goals for a while and keep the candle burning for as long as you can before extinguishing it or letting it burn itself out.

Spell Eight - new job, hate it spell
Oh dear! Sometimes, regardless of our best intentions, the new job we strove for is not what we imagined. We find out the hard way that the grass is definitely not greener on the other side. What can we do?

Buy a jasmine plant to keep indoors. Write down what is wrong with the job and what you need to change about it, if it can indeed be changed. Then say these words over the plant:

> *Lady Brighid, goddess of inspirations,*
> *Help me please.*
> *A career mistake I have made.*
> *Show me the right path in months of three.*
> *An' it harm none, so mote it be.*

When the flowers bloom on the plant, a new path will present itself to you - perhaps sooner than three months.

Spell Nine – an interview charm spell
So you are going to an interview. Make sure you wear something that you feel confident in and, if you can, wear a piece of turquoise jewellery or carry a piece in your pocket. Turquoise is

great for protection but it is also a good luck stone. It enhances communication and inspiration, which is certainly needed in some of today's challenging job interviews. Do this spell on a Wednesday. Hold the turquoise in your hand as you say:

> *Mighty Mercury, quick and wise,*
> *Help me to be the best surprise.*
> *The interviewers will hire me on the spot.*
> *They will know I am right for the job.*
> *Mighty Mercury, I will be the best interviewee.*
> *An' it harm none, so mote it be.*

Spell Ten - negative office spell
Despite our best intentions, some people just do not like us. Moreover, when you walk the path of the Craft you will become acutely aware of the atmosphere when you walk into a room. You will be able to feel the negative vibes straight away. One way to protect yourself is to imagine a mirrored cloak around you so that whatever comes your way is bounced right back to the sender.

However, there are other ways we can counteract negativity, such as this spell. Try and find some smoky quartz, either jewellery or simply a small piece. Nowadays, in many New Age shops you may find smoky quartz angels that can sit on your desk. This is a stone that can help to heal and to absorb negative energies. However, we need to give it some power before we take it into work. In the light of a silver candle, rub some frankincense oil onto the smoky quartz as you recite these words:

> *Smoky quartz, powers be.*
> *Absorb the painful negativity*
> *So that my place of work will be light and free.*
> *An' it harm none, so mote it be.*

Take the smoky quartz with you to work and leave it there all week. At the end of the week, take it home and soak it in some salt water overnight. Then do the ritual again over the weekend, ready for the next working week. Do this as often as you need to.

Spell Eleven – a promotion spell
You are doing a great job at work and really want that promotion. Show off your power and your light. Light a yellow candle. Write your prospective job on a piece of yellow card or paper and drip three drops of bergamot oil onto it, as you recite these words:

> *Father Jupiter, strong and bright,*
> *Let me show bosses my might.*
> *For the promotion I am right.*
> *Father Jupiter, blessed be.*
> *An' none shall it harm forever.*
> *So mote it be.*

Afterwards, fold up the paper or card three times and keep it in your drawer until you achieve your promotion. Then give thanks and rip the card up three times before throwing it away.

Spell Twelve – protection and clearing spell
This is a good spell to protect you at work or to 'clear the air'. Make up some holy water: magic sea salt and water, with three drops of frankincense oil. Shake it up and put it into a spray bottle. Before anyone gets into your place of work - or if you are the last to leave - spray around the office or wherever you are for the majority of time. Hold an obsidian crystal in your hand as you do so, and say:

> *Circle of protection, I invoke thee.*
> *Let me be safe and free,*
> *Encased within your loving embrace,*

> *Forever protected from those in this place.*
> *An' it harm none, so mote it be.*

Obsidian is a good stone to have at work as it sends negative thoughts on their way. However, you can also do this spell at home if you wish, covering yourself with protection in case you are confronted with something hurtful. Just change the spell to your individual situation.

Spell Thirteen - a horticulture spell
If you work in horticulture and have some problems with the plants, there are many appropriate spells, from blessing the soil or plants to creating magical compost. Witches have many spells for the Earth. As beings of nature we adhere to the rules and beliefs of Gaia, while the Green Man is also our brother, whom we respect. The very first spells were probably for nature, either to do with healing or with having a good harvest and a bountiful crop.

However, here we will concentrate on one particular aspect, developing plants to a full and longer-lasting bloom.

There are two crystals that are particularly good to work with in a horticultural setting. The first is moonstone, which helps gardeners to get their green fingers creating magic again. The other is malachite, which helps plants bloom longer. We use the fresh herbs tarragon and fennel. Place the stones (you can use both malachite and moonstone) on top of the fresh herbs. Say these words:

> *Light and dark, black and white,*
> *Let my garden bloom big and bright.*
> *Flowers and plants, large and small,*
> *Blessed be to one and all.*

Carry the stones in your pocket when you go to work, and put the herbs in the garden to heal the soil.

Spell Fourteen - a better communication spell

In our working lives there are often times when we wish we hadn't said something, while at other times we often have the answer but are afraid to speak up. This spell is basically a confidence spell, which I write about in the Family letter specifically for those taking exams. However, here we shall concentrate on communication particularly in relation to work.

The crystal that is really useful here is kunzite, which has excellent communication attributes. A piece of jade is also very good as a wisdom-bearing stone. We want to concentrate on opening up the throat chakra (the fifth energy centre), the link between ourselves and the world around us. It is the chakra connected with communication and self-expression. Any stone of blue or green colour will be right for this so sapphire, aquamarine and turquoise are also good here.

Light a silver candle and hold the stone in your hands. Imagine the light of the candle streaming into your throat, enhanced by the stone in your hands. Imagine a blockage in your throat being cleared and a pathway of blue light being reflected back into the silver candle. Start to whisper:

Let me speak confidently.
Blessed all, so mote it be.

Repeat it over and over again, getting louder each time until at last you say the words confidently and loudly. Take the stone or jewellery with you when you go to work.

Spell Fifteen - a legal spell

If you are a lawyer or work in a legal setting, the crystal for you is bloodstone. Jokes aside, this is a very powerful stone and often brings the owner victory in whatever dealings they have.

Light a red candle and say these words over the bloodstone on a Tuesday:

> *Hear me Mars, hear me Mars,*
> *Victory I do seek.*
> *In all my work, I beseech thee,*
> *Let me win, always victory.*
> *An' it harm none, so mote it be.*

Wear or keep the stone on your person in all your business dealings.

Spell Sixteen – a spell for health professionals

Everybody, no matter their role in life, needs a little boost. Health professionals and those who work in the caring professions also need a little help themselves now and again. This is a spell especially written for those who work in that arena. We shall ask Apollo for his help as he is one of the gods of medicine. He is also the sun god and we need his golden light of healing and warmth in our caring work.

Anoint or make a yellow candle with jasmine and rosemary oils. If making the candle, put in three drops of each oil. Recite this spell over the light of the candle:

> *Mighty Apollo, gracious golden sun,*
> *Help the healing ones,*
> *They who care for those in pain and need.*
> *Spread your warmth and care to them.*
> *May your strength power their pursuits.*
> *For now and evermore, blessed be.*
> *An' it harm none, so mote it be.*

Keep the candle burning as long as possible and meditate a while for all those who help the sick and needy.

Spell Seventeen – a retail charm spell

If you work in the retail sector, things may have been difficult in recent years. Other cultures have different ways of dealing with business problems and feng shui is sometimes consulted. Similarly, we are going to use a feng shui coin in our good luck charm; these are Chinese coins with a hole in the centre.

You will need red ribbon, an acorn painted gold, a feng shui coin and a piece of citrine. Drill a little hole in the citrine and also the acorn (if it is a real one. Better still, a golden acorn charm will usually have a loop on it already). Thread the three charms onto the red ribbon and secure them with a knot at both ends so they don't fall down the ribbon. Hang up your charm in your shop or place of work, saying these words:

> *Blessed Lakshmi, hear my plea,*
> *Goddess of wealth and prosperity.*
> *Help me in my pursuits.*
> *Help me to sell my goods.*
> *Great goddess Lakshmi, blessed be.*
> *An' it harm none, so mote it be.*

It would also be wise to put an image of an elephant or of an owl in your shop, as these are the symbols of Lakshmi.

Spell Eighteen – the candle and needle success spell

This is the time-honoured candle and needle spell which has been specially formulated with your career success in mind. Make an orange candle with jasmine, lemongrass and rosemary oils in it, or anoint a bought candle with these oils. Do this spell every night for a week, starting on a Thursday. Stick a needle halfway into the candle; when the flame burns down to the needle, the spell takes effect.

> *Success I seek in all my business.*
> *Business, success, victory.*
> *An' it harm none, so mote it be.*

Light the candle as you say these words and let the candle burn down to the needle, then extinguish it. Move the needle down a little further each day you do the spell and repeat it for the following seven nights until the candle finishes.

Spell Nineteen – the beat the recession spell
If you can have a plant in your place of work then buy a marigold or rosemary plant to keep there. Before taking the plant to work, say these words over it:

> *Blessed Juno, in times of strife,*
> *Let this plant help in my fight.*
> *Recession from these doors be gone.*
> *Blessed Juno, an' it harm none,*
> *So mote it be.*

Take the plant in to work and take care of it lovingly.

Spell Twenty – the good luck besom spell
This is a good luck charm to hang up above the door of your shop or workplace. You are going to make a small besom, or broom.

Go out for a walk in the park or in the woods and collect several fallen twigs. They only need to be about 10 to 15 cm long, with one longer and thicker. This will be the central twig which the others are attached to. Bring all the small twigs together and attach them around the central twig at one end, secured with an elastic band. Then tie a red ribbon round the elastic band to hide it. If you can, attach a little bell to it and also an acorn, painted gold.

> *Little good luck witch riding this broom,*
> *Luck and prosperity you bring to this room.*
> *Grant success in all I do.*
> *Little besom, blessed be.*
> *An' it harm none, for now and evermore,*
> *So mote it be.*

Hang the besom up above a door and occasionally dress it with fennel, dill, rosemary or jasmine flowers.

There, dear Reader, you have twenty spells for the career sector of your life. Always have a go at writing your own spells, using mine as a guide but changed to suit your own individual situation. No-one is better at sorting out your problems than you, so always trust your own instincts.

Blessed Be

More Career Correspondences

Herbs

Chamomile is a staple herb than can be used for so much, from teas to oils and cosmetics.

Comfrey is very good for skin complaints such as bruises, varicose veins and inflamed muscles.

Elder flower - The elder tree is sacred to us so never on any occasion destroy one. The flowers and fruit are so beneficial for us, with medicinal, culinary, cosmetic and household uses.

Mint is a fantastic herb for teas and essential oil; it is also an insect repellent.

Oregano or *wild marjoram* is another wonderful general purpose herb. A word of warning though: marjoram is not to be given to pregnant women, either in medicinal doses or as an essential oil, as it is a uterine stimulant.

Crystals

Amazonite is a great stone for self-expression, but be careful if in an argument with your boss! It can give you strength when making tough decisions.

Amber or 'gold of the north' is a wonderfully calming yet strong stone which reinforces your confidence when going into battle, as it were.

Aventurine is a lovely stone for the heart, so good for friendship and for eliminating anger. It is very useful in legal matters.

Goldstone is a great stone for success, prosperity and getting your wish granted.

Essential Oils

Jasmine oil is great for depression and fatigue, a very feminine oil.

Marigold or *calendula oil* has anti-inflammatory and antiseptic properties and is also antibacterial and antifungal, a truly magnificent plant. It can be made into an infusion by steeping the petals in warm vegetable oil.

Orange oil is a true all-rounder as it brings peace and calm to the body and mind while gently lifting the spirit.

Woodruff oil promotes harmony and psychic awareness.

Family

Dear Reader,

The family is a huge subject, with issues from fertility to protecting the home, from teenagers taking exams to moving to a new house, or even finding a new home. There are many spells and some are very ancient. The witch's protection jar for the family home is probably amongst the oldest of spells that have survived. Herbs were often hung at the doors to ward off evil spirits, and in later years the horseshoe also came to represent a force of goodwill for the owner of the house.

There are many gods and goddesses of hearth and home. Family, after all, is the central foundation of society. One to be called upon is Hestia, or her Roman equivalent Vesta. The hearth, or the eternal flame of the fire, is her symbol. The kitchen is of course sacred to her and in ancient times the fire of the home was never allowed to go out. In Norse religion, the goddess Frigg is patron of the home, being the wife of Odin. The English name Friday comes from the Anglo-Saxon version of her name, Frigge; so Friday is a good day for calling upon her. The other goddess to call upon is Juno, the patron of motherhood; you can call upon her if a problem involves children.

In ancient Rome, lares or familiars were called upon and homes had altars to the family guardians. The lares are often depicted as male in a tunic and with garlands adorning the head.

The colours corresponding to family are gold, silver, dark rose, lavender, black and brown. The oils we can use are lavender, iris, lily and peony among others. Other flowers and herbs to be used are angelica, hollyhock, Californian poppy and angel's trumpet. However, do not ingest or make oils with these as they are highly toxic; they are only for decorative purposes and for representing a specific god or goddess.

The number four is the appropriate number, for practicality and loyalty. So let us begin with a spell for the protection of the home.

Spell One – a home protection potion
4 cups of water
1 tsp vervain
1 tsp sea salt
1 tsp each frankincense and myrrh
1 pinch of wolf bane

Simmer the ingredients over a low flame for 15 minutes, then let the potion cool and put it into a jar. Sprinkle this potion when and wherever protection is needed, for example at the door and the windows as a psychic sealant.

Another form of protection for the home can be a lion! A real one may not be practical but symbolically the lion is regarded as regal and fearless, ruled by the sun and having great power. They are known to drive away evil spirits, so lions are often guardians of sacred places and will not allow any harmful force to enter the area they are asked to protect.

Spell Two – a protection for the home spell
Use a picture or ornament of a lion. Light a yellow candle and say over the lion:

> *Mighty lion, fierce and proud,*
> *Protect my home and grounds.*
> *Do not let enemies enter.*
> *Shelter all who live within.*

Blessed lion, gracious be.
An' it harm none, so mote it be.

Keep your lion in the hallway to guard your house.

Spell Three - holy water and magic salt spell

This is to clear the atmosphere of your home and to cast a protective spell around the house. First, create some magic salt by filling a bowl with sea salt and leaving it out in view of the full moon overnight. Store it in an airtight jar, tied with a white ribbon. Put four tablespoonfuls of your magic sea salt in a spray bottle with 400 ml of water and four drops of lavender oil. Shake it all up in the bottle and spray it around the house, going from room to room as you might with a sage stick. We are clearing the air and creating a peaceful atmosphere in the house. Say these words as you do so:

Blessed be to one and all in my home.
Let fighting and worry be gone.
Let love, light and peace
Forever be in my home.
An' it harm none, so mote is be.

You can do this spell every month or every time there is a festival of the year. A list of festivals and their corresponding spells is given later.

Spell Four - the moving spell

When you have found the house you want to move into, there is a lot to be done. Yet first we need to give thanks to the house we have lived in before, and also give thanks to the new house we will be moving to.

Light a brown candle, anointed with lavender oil, and say your thanking prayer while the candle is alight and while you pack your belongings.

Blessed Vesta, thank you for your care.
Thank you for your love in my home.
Thank you for all you do for my family.
Let our move to a new home be just as blessed.
Gracious Vesta, blessed be. So mote it be.

Good luck in your new home.

Spell Five – a fertility potion
Witches are often asked about this and there are many ancient spells regarding fertility.

1 pinch jasmine
1 pinch dried oak leaf
1 pinch rose petals
1 pinch marjoram

Mix them together with a pestle and mortar. Then grind the mixture into a fine powder and sprinkle it under the bed. With regards to the oak leaf, do not on any account pull the leaf off a tree. Look on the ground, as nature will have supplied one for you.

There are many old customs and traditions concerning fertility. One of them is to keep a cucumber in the bedroom, which was believed to increase fertility. Another saying, for a man to increase his virility, was that he needed to eat an egg every day for forty days. However to counteract this there is another saying, simply 'egg bound'! Another ancient English fertility spell for men is to do with walnuts and chestnuts, surprise surprise...

Spell Six – a male fertility potion
Steep five chestnuts in a pot of water for five hours. Then strain and bury the nuts outside, but keep the water and add it to your bath.

Spell Seven – another male fertility spell
This is a different and more modern version of the previous spell.

4 walnuts in their shells
4 walnuts without their shells
4 chestnuts
1 bowl of water

Put all the ingredients in the water and leave for one night in light of the full moon. While in the moonlight, say these words over the water:

> *Father Jupiter, blessed be.*
> *Grant me a healthy baby.*
> *Help me grow a loving family.*
> *An' it harm none, so mote it be.*

In the morning, bury the nuts and keep the water to use in your bath. Interestingly, in hoodoo or voodoo the black walnut is used for many spells including for fertility.

Spell Eight – a female fertility spell

> *Goddess Juno, mother of all,*
> *I ask you to help me.*
> *Help me to conceive.*
> *Goddess Juno, blessed be.*
> *A child I crave, so mote it be.*

Rub iris or lavender oil into a moonstone as you say these words. Keep the moonstone near your bed and have some fresh peony flowers in your bedroom too if possible. Allow three months for this spell. If you have not conceived by then, repeat the spell.

Spell Nine – the 'go head lice!' spell
One of the main problems with young children is the dreaded scratchy heads they get from time to time. Head lice like clean hair, so don't think that they're associated with dirty or unhygienic environments; nothing could be further from the truth. There are lotions that you can buy at your local pharmacy but here is a potion from the past.

Castor oil was used in ancient Egypt to rid one of head lice, and it was also used as a hair restorer. Start with 50 ml of castor oil in a bottle. Put 10 drops of tea tree essential oil, 10 drops of lavender essential oil, 5 drops of peppermint oil and 5 drops of bergamot oil into the castor oil and shake it all up. Name and date the potion. As you shake it all up, say this spell:

> *Little mites be gone.*
> *Let this spell send you on the run.*
> *Stay away from my little one.*
> *So mote it be.*

Then massage the oil into the dry hair and leave it on for a good hour if you can. Make sure you massage the oil behind the ears and everywhere on the child's head. Start to comb out the lice with the oil still on. Then use cool water to wash everything away and an antiseptic shampoo in a final wash. Do this for seven nights, depending on the severity of the infestation.

If you have never used any of these oils on a child before, do a little skin test first. Dab a little of the mixture on the back, just below the neck and wait for twenty-four hours to see if there is a reaction before applying to the head. If the child is allergic to any of the essential oils, you can omit or change the quantities. Or you could be completely original and do exactly what the ancient Egyptians did; just use castor oil on the head and comb the little bugs out.

Another oil that was used in ancient Egypt for the removal of head lice was moringa. It was also applied neat on the skin to prevent mosquito bites. The past always has something to teach us.

Spell Ten – the mother's help spell
Here is a spell especially for mums whose children are behaving, well, like children, but your patience has completely worn thin. Make yourself a cup of bergamot tea (in other words, Earl Grey). Bergamot is a wonderful plant that can help with treating anything from depression to stomach complaints.

Light a gold candle which has been anointed with four drops of bergamot oil. While sipping the tea, say these words:

> *Oh goddess Juno, ruler of money and motherhood.*
> *Help me to be patient with my brood.*
> *Their bedrooms are a mess.*
> *Their nagging a constant pest.*
> *Help me to restore balance and tranquillity*
> *In my home and with my family.*
> *An' it harm none, so mote it be.*

Sit for a while just sipping the tea and meditating on the flame of the candle. Perform this spell anytime you feel you need to.

Spell Eleven – an exam confidence spell
Exams can be horrible and predominantly it is the young who go through them. So much stress is put upon them, with so many hopes and dreams for the desired outcome. There are quite a number of things you can do. Thyme was used in ancient times to encourage bravery, so you could use it in food for those taking exams.

Perform this spell on a Wednesday. Gather the herbs thyme, lavender, oregano and mint. Write out this spell and say these words:

> *Ancestors of my family,*
> *Help my child in the days ahead.*

They worry and their exams are a dread.
Let them be brave and true.
Let the answers come through.
Let their pen answer wisely.
An' it harm none, so mote it be.

Light a silver candle and sprinkle the herbs over the spell that you have written down. Then roll up the paper with the herbs inside and secure it with some blue ribbon so that it looks like a scroll. Keep it in a safe place. When the results come through, give thanks to your ancestors then burn the scroll and bury the remains in a garden.

Spell Twelve – the witch's protection jar spell
The witch's jars and bottles which can be used today in houses are not curses or evil. They are for the protection of the house and all those within. Many of the jars in the old days would have had nails in them because nails were then made of iron. Iron is a highly regarded metal for getting rid of spirits and it can ward off evil.

Also in the bottles one would find pieces of fingernail or hair, the witch giving something of herself to the universe in protecting the house. This is a similar idea to money bag spells of yore, where a piece was given freely for the spell to take effect. In this spell, however, the Craft has changed with time. We are going to make a house protection bottle, but not with our nails or hair (unless you want to).

1 clove of garlic
1 bay leaf
1 basil leaf
1 tsp dill seeds
1 sage leaf
1 star anise
1 tsp black pepper
1 tsp fennel

1 tsp vervain
1 tbsp of magic sea salt

Put all the ingredients in a glass jar with an airtight lid, saying:

> *Garlic, bay, basil, dill, sage,*
> *Star anise, pepper black,*
> *Fennel, salt of the sea and vervain,*
> *Protect all in my domain.*
> *Salt and herbs, ten times ten,*
> *Guard now and evermore my den.*
> *It is done, an' it harm none.*
> *Blessed be, so mote it be.*

Ideally the jar would have been bricked up while the house was being built. But just keep it in a safe place where you can always see it - on a high kitchen shelf perhaps?

Spell Thirteen – a happy marriage spell
There are many marriage spells and there is even a recipe for a happy marriage cake. Write out ten points of what in your view a happy marriage needs; for example, equality, respect, sense of humour etcetera. Study them after you have written them down and roll the paper up in your hand like a scroll. Light a dark red candle and say these words:

> *Jupiter and Juno, blessed be.*
> *Help my marriage to be happy.*
> *Love and affection fill every room.*
> *Kind and loving we both shall be.*
> *Let our voices each be heard.*
> *Equal two parts of the one.*
> *An' it harm none,*
> *So mote it be.*

Then, holding the scroll, carefully burn it.

Spell Fourteen – a 'help me survive the holidays!' spell

Whether it is the summer holidays or Christmas, any length of time as the family winds down for a holiday season, there will be days fraught with "I'm bored" and "It's not fair" heard throughout the house. Try to limit those days with this spell at the beginning of the holidays. Make a silver candle with lavender and sage oils in it, and a gold candle with bergamot and rosemary oils in it. Light the candles and say these words:

> *Blessed be to candle light.*
> *Let my children not fight.*
> *The holidays are upon us.*
> *Let them be full of fun and creativity.*
> *My children will play good.*
> *They will be joyous and happy.*
> *No more my miserable brood.*
> *Candle light, blessed be.*
> *An' it harm none, so mote it be.*

Throughout the holidays, whenever you need to recharge, light the candles when the children have gone to bed and it is peaceful, and repeat the spell.

Spell Fifteen – a pregnancy stone spell

This is a spell for expectant mothers who are worried or anxious. One of the stones that is perfect for expectant mothers is red jasper, a stability gemstone that eases emotional stresses. It helps to balance the emotional energy in the body and it also promotes physical energy, so it is very good to have around. In addition, it is also very lucky for actors!

Light a dark red candle and, holding the jasper in your hands, say these words:

> *Mother Juno, blessed be.*
> *Help me to have a healthy pregnancy.*

> *Please take stress and anxiety away from me.*
> *An' it harm none, so mote it be.*

Leave the stone near your bed at night and keep it with you throughout the day, carrying it in your purse.

Spell Sixteen - the argument spell

This spell is all about making up after an argument. In families, it is inevitable that there will be arguments. Candles have a calming effect so you're going to use a specific candle and light it to clear the air. Make a lavender coloured candle with four drops of lavender oil in it. As you make the candle, say over it:

> *Candle fire, candle bright,*
> *Ease our arguments this night.*
> *Differences make constant fights.*
> *Help us to see*
> *The love between my partner and me.*
> *An' it harm none, so mote it be.*

When you and your partner are together, light the candle and talk things through.

Spell Seventeen – a something lost spell

There are times when items go missing for no apparent reason. Keys or jewellery, even things that you may have just put down, simply disappear. It's so frustrating. It could be absent mindedness but others would believe that it's the mischievous work of real entities. This is a little spell to be said when you are hunting round the house trying to find that lost item. Say it in every room and say it clearly so the little sprites can hear you! (A full description of the elementals can be found in *Spirit in the City*.)

> *Little sprites, I beseech thee,*
> *Bring back my ...(lost item)... to me.*
> *Little sprites, so mote it be.*

Spell Eighteen – the break a spell spell
Sometimes it feels as if we are cursed, that someone has put a spell on us. You will need a black candle and a mirror to break this. The spell is to be done in a protected circle of salt. Light the candle and look into the mirror, saying these words:

> *I send this magic back*
> *Through the candle black.*
> *Go now from this place.*
> *Never return to this face.*
> *Mirror blessed, I beseech,*
> *Cloak of mirrors cover me.*
> *An' it harm none, so mote it be.*

Keep staring into the mirror and imagine the curse or spell being lifted from you. Extinguish the flame, but not by blowing it out. Wrap the mirror up and, if you can, keep it especially for magical work.

Spell Nineteen - the happy families spell
Have a bouquet of flowers in the house of angel's trumpet, hollyhock, peony and iris. Place the flowers all around the house.

Make a gold candle with two drops of rosemary essential oil and two drops of lavender essential oil in it, or anoint a bought gold candle with these oils. Spray your holy water (see Spell Three) around the house to create a clear and harmonious atmosphere. After you have done this, light the candle and say these words:

> *Blessed be to my family,*
> *Forever strong and healthy.*
> *Blessed be to be forever happy.*
> *An' it harm none, so mote it be.*

Afterwards, open all the windows no matter how cold and let the air into every room. Breathe in the freshness and imagine the air bringing with it happy, positive energies.

Spell Twenty - family wishes spell
If you manage to go away on holiday to the beach, collect as many sea shells as you can together. When you come home, cut some stiff cardboard into a heart shape and glue the sea shells on both front and back. Make a little hole at the top for a piece of ribbon to go through, as you are going to hang up your wishes so you can see them all year round. Depending on how many sea shells you collected, you could make more hearts and hang them together. In the middle of each, write the word WISH on the shells. Now hang the hearts up and as you do so say these words:

I wish I may, I wish I might,
Let my family have their wish this night.
Blessed be to one and all. So mote it be.

Then throughout the year, when the family needs a little boost, touch the hearts and remember your holiday and how happy you all were.

There are many other spells for family, such as for sibling rivalry or babies that continuously cry. Witches have been mothers for years. Indeed many spells have been passed down through the centuries from women who were healers and midwives. We have touched upon some health spells here, such as for anxiety, fertility and pregnancy. However, the next letter is dedicated completely to certain common health conditions that we all suffer from.

Blessed Be

More Family Correspondences

Herbs

Acorns can be used for protection, strength, success, stability, healing and fertility.

Bay laurel (also *garlic*) is good for protection and good luck.

Carrot seed helps with fertility

Sage can clear the atmosphere in the home of any evil feeling. Other methods are the ringing of a bell, and using magic salt and holy water.

Vervain is a powerful all-purpose herb.

Crystals

Falcon's eye for boosting sexuality and encouraging pregnancy (and for sunburn!).

Jade for fertility, and also great for challenging situations and protection; it was once known as the Warrior's Stone.

Orange calcite for sexuality and confidence; it is also a good stone for students studying science.

Red jasper for convalescence and pregnancy.

Sardonyx for strength, protection and a happy marriage.

Essential Oils

Cinnamon oil is antibacterial and antifungal; it also helps to deaden the nerve where there is toothache.

Lettuce oil promotes male fertility. Lettuce was sacred to Min, the Egyptian god of fertility.

Health

Dear Reader,

As previously stated, many herbal remedies come from the past and have been passed through the generations. Indeed, my father believed that every illness known or unknown could be cured by a plant - we just have to find them.

But the remedies and spells here are only a guide. Always consult a medical practitioner or pharmacist if symptoms persist. Moreover, if you are already consulting a doctor, tell them that you intend to use herbal remedies and check whether these are fine alongside your conventional medication. Always listen to the doctor and never change your prescription.

The colours blue and white predominate with health work. Also in health we take note of the chakras (energy centres) and their own colours come into play. Every area of the body is governed by a colour according to the chakra system. There are seven of these centres, from the base of the spine to the top of the head. The base chakra is a deep red while the sacral, the area of sexuality, is orange; your solar plexus is yellow and the heart chakra is green; the throat chakra is blue, the colour of communication, the brow chakra is indigo and lastly the crown chakra is a violet colour.

Furthermore, each of the zodiac signs rules a certain part of the body:

Aries   - the head and brain
Taurus   - the throat

Gemini   - the lungs and nervous system
Cancer   - the stomach and breasts
Leo   - the heart area
Virgo   - the abdomen
Libra   - the kidneys and lower back
Scorpio   - the sex organs
Sagittarius - the hips and thighs
Capricorn   - the skeleton, teeth and skin
Aquarius   - the circulatory system
Pisces   - the feet and the lymphatic system

However, this does not necessarily mean that the specified parts are 'susceptible' to those particular zodiac signs or that they are weak spots. Indeed, it can mean that these are key areas that have extra strength; for example, Pisceans are the natural born dancers of the zodiac. In addition, there are herbs associated with these signs, a list of which can be found in the Correspondences section after this letter.

The gods and goddesses that can be called upon in health matters are Apollo and his son Asclepius, Artemis, Brighid and Eir, a Norse goddess who is the designated spirit of medicine, in particular women's health. Febris, too, was the Roman goddess of fever, so she is useful to know and we can also call upon Raphael who is the angel of healing.

When it comes to herbs and oils, basically every one is useful in health. Indeed, one could say that this is their primary purpose.

Spell One - the menopause spell
There are many ways in which nature helps us with this. Pomegranates are good, as are cranberries, so you could make a pomegranate and cranberry punch and drink it throughout the day. But when it comes to the menopause every woman is different. Some sail through the menopause without a thought while others turn into Medusa.

Here is a spell especially written for those women who are suffering with this natural aspect of being a woman. Light one red candle and one blue candle and say these words:

> *Blessed Hera, hear my plea,*
> *Grant me patience and understanding towards my family.*
> *Feelings of anger towards my husband have I.*
> *Hot flushes, changes, constant fight.*
> *Blessed Hera, cool my temper and my body.*
> *An' it harm none, so mote it be.*

Spell Two – for a sore throat (the magic gargle spell)
There are many remedies for sore throats. It is related to the blue chakra and therefore a blue candle is required (blue also being a natural healing colour). Agate is a good stone to use for sore throats, so we are going to make a gargle mixture with it. Take a piece of agate and drop it into some drinking water. Over the water, say or whisper:

> *Blessed agate, heal me please.*
> *My throat is sore and full of pain.*
> *Let me not have this again.*
> *Blessed agate, take away my sore throat.*
> *Blessed be. So mote it be.*

Then take out the stone and put a teaspoonful of your magic sea salt into the water and mix it in. Gargle with the water as often as you can. You could also make agate water. Just use drinking water and drop the agate in, leave it for about ten minutes and then take it out. You can sip the water all day. Always make sure that your agate is clean before you begin making any elixirs. (An elixir is exactly what you have just made by dropping the stone into the water.)

Spell Three – an arthritis pain spell
This is probably one of the worst types of pain to suffer from. It is a constant pain that never leaves us and we are always aware of it. There are a number of crystals that can help with arthritis: green aventurine, apatite and chrysoprase. See if you can find a piece of jewellery, such as a bracelet, made out of chrysoprase. Then light a purple candle and hold the crystal in your hands as you ask the angel Raphael:

> *Blessed Raphael, hear me please,*
> *Heal my pain with your touch.*
> *Angel Raphael, thank you. Blessed be.*

Keep holding the stone and place it on the part that hurts. If you have a piece of chrysoprase jewellery, then keep wearing it. Every so often, recharge the crystal or jewellery with this ritual.

Spell Four - the 'heal my heart of grief' spell
Grief is a condition that affects people in many different ways. There is the emotional pain but also a physical aspect to it. After a loved one has passed, for example, the traditional mourning period used to be a year but in our modern times we are lucky to be allowed a few days off work. However, life goes back to normal - or does it? In a period of grieving, we ourselves can suffer from numerous ailments that previously we would have recovered from easily. But now it may take weeks, so we need to heal the body too.

Make a white candle with lily oil in it, at the time of a full moon. Light the candle and say these words:

> *Gracious Mother, heal my heart.*
> *A loved one has passed.*
> *Heart, body and mind*
> *Need strength, love in kind.*
> *Gracious Mother, hear my spell,*

Make my body well.
Gracious Mother, blessed be.
An' it harm none, so mote it be.

Meditate on the candle and let its warmth penetrate into your heart.

Spell Five – a depression spell

Depression is like a wave that sweeps over us and those who suffer from it often find no release. The best thing is to follow your instincts. If you're tired, then sleep. Relax, meditate and pamper yourself. Look after yourself. Treat yourself like a god or goddess; you are divine and unique after all.

Put two drops each of lavender, juniper, rose, clove and bay essential oils into your bath water. Soak in the water and relax. Imagine a white light of healing emanating from the water. When you get out of the bath, imagine that feeling of the water still comforting you and say:

Sacred waters, send me release
From this sadness and depression.
Sacred waters, let my illness heal.
Sacred waters, blessed be. So mote it be.

When you feel the depression sweeping over you again, remember the warm comforting bath and say the spell again.

Spell Six – a sleep spell

In our very busy world it can be difficult to switch off. There are a number of things that can help. Howlite is a good crystal, while the herb jasmine encourages sweet dreams and passion flower brings a deep peaceful sleep. Hold a piece of howlite and rub two drops of jasmine essential oil into it as you say:

Sleep, sleep, sleep come to me.
Sleep, sleep, sleep. So mote it be.

Keep the jasmine under your pillow and allow yourself to drift off. Surprisingly, peppermint tea can also aid insomnia.

Spell Seven – a period pain spell
Lavender oil is good for period pain when massaged into the stomach. Aquamarine can also help with hormonal problems and period pain. Make yourself some rosemary tea: boil the water and pour it over a couple of fresh sprigs of rosemary, leave it for five minutes and then sweeten it with honey. Rosemary is a very versatile herb and can regulate the menstrual cycle. Liquorice tea is another that can improve digestion and also soothe menstrual pain.

Rub some liquorice oil into an aquamarine stone, then hold it over your body where you have the pain while saying this spell:

> *Mother Goddess, such pain have I.*
> *From month to month, suffer do I.*
> *Help me please, from month to month.*
> *An' it harm none, so mote it be.*

Spell Eight – a stomach upset spell
Ginger tea is always good for getting rid of sickness and that horrible nausea, especially of morning sickness. Just grind the root up and use it in a tea by adding hot water. Liquorice is excellent for constipation.

Further, for the sickly or acid stomach that accompanies IBS, eating one or two fresh basil leaves really works. Peppermint can also alleviate a stomach upset. However, if you have a constantly sick stomach you should see a doctor first.

It might also be an idea to rebalance the chakra points of the lower body. The stone beryl can help to heal and regulate the base, solar plexus, stomach and breast chakras. Infuse a piece of beryl or beryl jewellery with some ginger oil. While rubbing the ginger oil into the beryl, say these words:

> *Stomach upsets be gone.*
> *Sickness and heartburn be free.*
> *An' it harm none, so mote it be.*

Hold the stone over your stomach or wear the beryl jewellery every day.

Spell Nine – a headache spell
Headaches are horrible gnawing pains that never seem to stop. As we use so much energy rushing here and there, it is inevitable that everyone from time to time will suffer with a headache. However, instead of reaching for the pills try these remedies and this spell.

Surprisingly, lemons are renowned for their healing properties. The first thing to try is a cup of bergamot (Earl Grey) tea with a slice of lemon in it and see if that helps. Or you could cut the rind off a lemon, mash it into a paste and apply it to your forehead; if you have some already prepared and kept in the fridge, it would be nice and cool when you need it. If however the pain is too great to be messing around with making a paste, then cut two slices of lemon and apply them to the temples while saying these words:

> *Eir, hear me please,*
> *Let my pain ease.*
> *Take away the pain in my head.*
> *I do not want to spend the day in bed.*
> *Blessed Eir, hear me please.*
> *An' it harm none, so mote it be.*

If you can, lie down for a while with the lemon slices on your forehead. But if you have repeated headaches, please see a doctor.

Spell Ten – a fever spell

Fevers often accompany a virus illness and the fever is the first indication that something is wrong. Febris is the Roman goddess of fevers. There are many things we can do with fevers now: taking aspirin or paracetamol, keeping well hydrated by drinking water, wearing very light clothing and keeping the air circulating. As always, rest is best. Many fevers last up to three days and the temperature can rise two or three degrees. While resting, say this little spell:

> *Goddess Febris, blessed be,*
> *Please take care of me.*
> *This fever will break and I will be well.*
> *Goddess Febris, please hear my spell.*
> *So mote it be.*

Spell Eleven – a toothache spell

Toothache is possibly the worst pain you can ever have, along with a fear of going to the dentist. There are many gels and sprays we can put on our teeth and gums to help them while waiting to see a dentist. However, there are a couple of herbal remedies for the temporary solution of toothache. One of them involves onions.

Despite the smell, onions actually have antibacterial properties. Therefore, chewing a raw one will kill any germs in the mouth. A piece of amber, jet or malachite is also good; rub some clove oil into any of these stones. As you do so, say these words:

> *Toothache be gone.*
> *An' it harm none,*
> *So mote it be.*

Then hold the stone over the side of your mouth where the pain is. You could also sleep with the stone under your pillow.

Spell Twelve – a bad back massage oil

There are many things we can do. First, let's make a massage oil. Make up a 50 ml batch with a carrier oil such as sweet almond, and use four drops each of chamomile, rosemary, ginger and lavender essential oils.

Then put a couple of drops of lavender and eucalyptus oils into the bath water and relax in the water before drying off and applying the massage oil. Afterwards, rest and meditate upon your back. Imagine a lavender colour, warming and healing, swirling into your back and taking the pain away.

Spell Thirteen - for a friend in need

Make a blue candle with lavender, cedar and geranium oils in it. When the candle is ready, push a needle halfway into it. Whatever the complaint of your friend, write it down and sprinkle some lavender over the words. Then light the candle and say:

> *My friend ...(name)... is in need.*
> *Please, universe, give her strength,*
> *Let her pain be gone.*
> *An' it harm none.*
> *Universe, blessed be.*
> *So mote it be.*

You can repeat this spell each night while your friend is suffering. Each time the candle burns down to the needle, extinguish it and move the needle further down when the candle is cold.

Spell Fourteen – a child illness spell

Child illnesses are a worry, and if any symptoms linger or you are worried always consult a doctor. Let your instincts be your guide. But there are a couple of other things you can do. For example, with skin ailments such as measles or chickenpox you can treat the itching with chamomile lotion. Other illnesses can be very frightening for young children who may have not been ill before, so this is a little spell for children who are frightened:

> *Goddess Brighid, I beseech,*
> *Let my child be well.*
> *Heal her wounds and dry her tears.*
> *Let her fight this illness with your strength.*
> *Goddess Brighid, hear my spell.*
> *Gracious Brighid, blessed be.*
> *An' it harm none, so mote it be.*

Spell Fifteen – an acne spell
First, make up a skin wash with two drops of calendula flower oil and then a thyme water rinse. Check your proprietary facial wash to see if it already has calendula in it - you may be surprised. To make the thyme water, boil some water and pour it over some fresh thyme; then bottle it and keep it for rinsing.

Now take an egg and clean it by making a hole at the top and bottom of the egg and blowing the insides out. Then wash the egg out and leave it to dry. Sprinkle some thyme, lavender and dandelion into the egg, and say these words:

> *Universe, set me free.*
> *Take away this acne.*
> *The egg that breaks,*
> *My acne will take.*
> *An' it harm none,*
> *So mote it be.*

Then bury the egg in a garden; when the egg disintegrates down into the earth, the acne will go.

There are also teas you can use such as dandelion and burdock, which helps the body to release its toxins, skin bacteria and excess hormones, all of which causes acne.

HEALTH | 95

Spell Sixteen – for vomiting (the magic stomach powder)
As previously mentioned, ginger is always best for stomach upsets. However, there is an old eastern remedy which, apparently, was even known in King Solomon's time. It calls for cinnamon and cardamom.

Use three cinnamon sticks and one teaspoon of ground cardamom, and grind them all together in a pestle and mortar to create a powder. Keep this powder in a special bottle, labelled and dated. Pour boiling water over a teaspoonful of the stomach powder in a cup, and sip it slowly to bring relief.

Spell Seventeen – a detox magic sea salt scrub
You are going to make a sea salt scrub, preferably use your magic salt. You also need sweet almond oil, wheat germ oil, coconut oil, jojoba seed oil, evening primrose oil and rice bran oil. Rice bran is a lovely light oil and is extremely moisturising and refreshing to the skin.

The salt is the base but it needs to be completely covered and soaked by the oils, which are used in equal amounts. When you have put all the ingredients together, mix them up well with a spoon. In your bath, rub some of the scrub onto yourself to clear away dead skin then wash it off with water. You should be left silky and smooth. Keep the rest of the scrub in an airtight jar.

Spell Eighteen – a magic dehydration drink
Dehydration can sweep upon us very quickly if we're busy and forget to drink enough water; this can upset the natural balance of minerals, sugar and salts in our bodies. One of the key indicators of dehydration is feeling thirsty and lightheaded. However, with babies and children the condition is more serious and we need to be extremely vigilant as they can become dehydrated very quickly, so always consult a doctor if in doubt.

If you are dehydrated you need to drink plenty of fluids, but not just water as that will further dilute the minerals in the body. Take other fluids such as fruit juices. Here is a special rehydration solution:

1 pint of drinking water
½ tsp baking soda
½ tsp magic sea salt
4 tbsp sugar

Mix all the ingredients until dissolved and drink small amounts, taking slow sips now and again.

Spell Nineteen – a magic sunburn lotion spell
There are many remedies for sunburn but sunstroke is terrible, so always be sensible in the sun. However, if you have a mild case of sunburn here are a couple of remedies. One of the main ones is natural yoghurt which can be used as a cream. You can also apply a compress of vinegar and cucumber juice, or even cold tea.

For a special lotion, use 4 tsp of lemon juice, 8 tsp of sweet almond oil, 2 tsp of honey (preferably clear) and 1 tsp of water. Put all the ingredients in a screw-top jar and shake it well. As you do so, say these words:

> *Dear Apollo, god of the sun,*
> *Forgive me for I have been too long*
> *In your watchful gaze.*
> *I long to be outside for days and days.*
> *Forgive me, Apollo, and help me please.*
> *Send me sunburn ease.*
> *An' it harm none, so mote it be.*

Apply it thoroughly and, if you can stand it, massage the oil into your skin.

Spell Twenty – a sore feet lotion

Poor feet, we are on them all day and we never really care for them. Here are a couple of remedies for sore feet.

If you have some yellow discolouration on your toenails, you may have a fungal infection. If so, make a foot soak with four drops each of thyme and marigold oils in warm water and soak the feet. Afterwards, dry the feet well and apply a couple of drops of tea tree oil to each toenail and rub it in.

To make magic sea salt foot soak, put a tablespoonful of your magic sea salt and two drops each of lavender and rose essential oils in a bowl of water. Let the feet soak in this.

There are countless other spells for various ailments. However, I reiterate that you should trust your instincts - pain is always a warning – and consult a doctor if something is wrong. Have a check-up every so often. The times we live in are indeed very stressful so try to find time for yourself.

Blessed Be

More Health Correspondences

Herbs
In addition to the herbs already mentioned, here are the designated herbs for each star sign:

Aries - honeysuckle, cowslip, rosemary
Taurus - elder, lovage, spearmint
Gemini - lavender, hare's foot, fern
Cancer - saxifrage, hyssop, balm
Leo - bay, borage, angelica
Virgo - caraway, myrtle, fennel
Libra - daisy, garden mint
Scorpio - broom, hops, basil
Sagittarius - moss, sage, dandelion
Capricorn - comfrey, hemlock, beet
Aquarius - sorrel, quince, heart's ease
Pisces - dock, sage, fig

Chamomile is good for relaxing the nervous system.

Eucalyptus can rejuvenate the body and spirit.

Raspberry leaf can be combined in equal part with cut *ginger root* to make a tea; having steeped, this can be sipped slowly to end a fit of sneezing.

Essential Oils
Aloe vera, ginseng, horsetail and *myrrh* are all excellent healing oils.

Patchouli oil is used for balance and confidence.

Crystals

Amber is good for the solar plexus, therefore healing the immune system, the digestion, asthma, depression and influenza.

Bloodstone can boost the immune system and aid self-protection.

Howlite is a calming stone, often used to help with insomnia.

Lepidolite is also said to aid sleep - pop a piece under your pillow.

Merlinite is an ideal stone for healing and for meditation.

Black and White Magic

Dear Reader,

At times we have used black candles, but this is not 'black magic'! The important issue with spell-weaving is to use the correct correspondences, and to have the right focus and the right intentions. Our creed dictates that we do not harm another living being. We embrace all and this includes the dark - at times we need to enter the world of the dark in order to bring light.

Therefore, there really is no difference between light and dark magic. The media image of the 'white witch' and the 'dark priestess' is precisely that, a media misconception to titillate and entertain. Of course, there are those who follow the dark arts but even in their cupboards and on their altars there will be white candles, and we all use the same oils, herbs and crystals. We are the same except that those practitioners who work against the natural order of things, or who try to manipulate others against their free will, are focussing on the negative aspects of the Craft.

Spells such as for death, hurt, nightmares and revenge are negative and regarded as the dark part of the Craft; not black, just in the shadows as it were. Whereas spells such as for enchantment, healing, dreams and fertility are positive and are firmly in the light part of the Craft.

Spells weave through space and time. They are the knowledge of and reverence for the ancestors, combined with magic and nature; never bending the will but tapping into the power of nature and always in return helping nature. For example, at times we need to send something back to someone who may wish us ill. This is not dark magic, but protection not only for ourselves but also for our loved ones. Sometimes it just has to be done.

Happy spell-weaving! Cast spells with a conscience and you will not go wrong.

Blessed Be

Spells for the Seasons of the Year

Dear Reader,

We have looked at the most common subjects for spells. However, there are certain festival times of the year when specific spells can be cast.

We shall start with our New Year, Samhain, more commonly known as Hallowe'en, on October 31st. This is a perfect time to do spells regarding loved ones who have passed away. The veil between the worlds is thin now. You could look into your magic mirror, or do this spell for inviting your loved ones to visit you in a dream. Before you go to sleep, say this spell:

> *Ancestors of my past,*
> *Please come to me at last.*
> *Visit me in my dream this night.*
> *But please do not give me a fright.*
> *An' it harm none, so mote it be.*

The next festival is that of Yule, on December 21st. This is a time when you can make a health spell, since it is winter - any spell to do with either physical, mental or spiritual health. Here is an example. Light a green candle anointed with pine essential oil, and say:

> *Season of winter, you bring many changes.*
> *Season of winter, blessed be.*

Please do not bring sickness to me.
Season of winter, let me be well.
Season of winter, hear my spell.
An' it harm none, so mote it be.

Next we have Imbolc, on the 2nd of February. The turning of the wheel has begun and after this date there is a quickening of life. So this is a good time to do spells regarding fertility. Jade is a good stone to be used and parsley the right herb. Rub some parsley oil onto a piece of jade and keep the stone always nearby while trying to conceive.

Ostara is on the 21st of March, a time for blessing the soil and compost, for planting and getting the ground ready for the new, fresh herbs and flowers of the summer.

Herbs and food within this garden grow,
Drink of nature's bounty well.
Grow strong, thanks be to this spell.
Grow into nourishing food
So that you will taste good.
Blessed be to plant and soil.
You grow with my toil.
Thanks be to nature.
Thanks be to all nature, sun, rain and bees.
An' it harm none, so mote it be.

The festival of Beltane comes on April 30th. Traditionally we also celebrate the 1st of May (with maypoles) and this is a perfect time to perform spells to do with sex magic. As sex magic is unique to the individuals concerned, try writing your own personal spells. The specific colours to be used are of course red, orange and yellow. The oils are cinnamon, rose and sandalwood. The crystals are citrine and diamond. Enjoy and use them wisely!

The next festival is the summer solstice, or Litha, on June 21st. This is a perfect time for love spells, so ask Cupid and

Aphrodite (Venus) to help in matters of the heart. Soul mate spells are also good at this time. Take a piece of jewellery that you like the most; we are going to enchant it using the magic of this powerful midsummer night. Lighting one red and one yellow candle, place your piece of jewellery in between the two candles and say these words:

> *Midsummer magic, midsummer madness,*
> *Grant me a wish this night.*
> *Make my jewellery twinkle with fairy might.*
> *He who looks upon this jewellery*
> *Will fall in love with me.*
> *Fairy magic, come to me.*
> *Grant this wish for me.*
> *Blessed be to all fairies.*
> *An' it harm none, so mote it be.*

The next festival is the first of the autumn. It is on the 2nd of August and called Lammas. This is a good time to do a spell for travelling, as many people will be going on their summer holidays. Here is a travelling spell:

> *Travelling here, travelling there,*
> *Travelling absolutely everywhere.*
> *Blessed Mercury, keep me safe*
> *In all my travels wherever I am bound.*
> *By sea, in the air or on the ground.*
> *An' it harm none, so mote it be.*

Travel with a piece of turquoise jewellery on you, or carry a piece of turquoise in a bag or purse. This is the stone of protection when travelling.

Mabon is a wonderful time of the year, the harvest festival found on or around September 22nd. This is the last of the eight festivals of the year for us, as the wheel starts turning once again at Samhain. At Mabon the fruit is ripe, the harvest is well under way and we are beginning to think of the coming winter. (While for those in the southern hemisphere it is the exciting time that accompanies the coming of summer.) This festival is the marker of past, present and future, so spells of time are perfect at Mabon - either blessings and gratitude for the past year or the creation of a spell for the future. Light one black and one white candle and say these words:

> *Changing seasons, seasons past,*
> *Let the future hold what's true at last.*
> *Let all my dreams come true.*
> *Let all my adventures be new.*
> *Blessed Mabon, let it be.*
> *An' it harm none, so mote it be.*

Think of five things that have happened to you in the year since last Samhain, then list five goals you wish for in the coming year and write them all down on a piece of yellow paper. Afterwards, keep the paper in a safe place and next Mabon you can take it out and see what you have accomplished. Give thanks and burn the paper as you repeat the Mabon future spell above.

There is an in-depth description of all the festivals in *The Craft in the City*.

Blessed Be

The Last Word

Dear Reader,

We have now come to the end of our journey with spells and spell-weaving. I do hope you have learned some of the correspondences. Use them and try to write your own spells, thinking of the correspondences as pieces of thread that you are going to use to weave your own magic. Your spells are your own creation. Some can rhyme but they do not have to. You can honour the gods, or just the universe. Remember always to write down all your spells and magical work in your Book of Shadows.

Dear Reader, it is YOU who is in control of your magic. Use the Craft wisely and responsibly - and be careful what you cast for.

Blessed Be

Publications in this Series

Previous Publications...

The Craft in the City (ISBN 978-1-907203-43-5)
The Witch in the City (ISBN 978-1-907203-63-3)

Still to come in this Series

Magic in the City
The different forms of magic in the city, focusing on English and Celtic magic, and looking at the different practices and traditions. Also includes masks, astral projection, the zodiac and the Magical Battle of Britain.

Spirit in the City
The supernatural entities that we work with. The elementals of earth, fire, air and water.